How to Learn Microsoft Access VBA Programming Quickly!

COPYRIGHT

Chapter One
Introduction to Databases and Microsoft Access

A database is a collection of information stored somewhere for easy organization and exploration. Databases are used in various situations such as keeping a record of friends, registering employees job attendance, counting the number of students in a classroom and keeping a record of their grades. This means that we have been using databases all our life.

We are going to learn how to use the computer to create and exploit databases. We will use Microsoft Access. Learning how to use Microsoft Access and some programming is just a matter of applying your already tremendous knowledge on information storage and retrieval.

Microsoft Access is a software product used for desktop database applications. You can use it for personal stuff, for home, or for your business/company.

We are going to learn not only how to create databases in Microsoft Access, but also add some programming to further tell the computer what to do with data we provide.

To further enhance the functionality of our databases in Microsoft Access, we will learn Visual Basic for Applications, a programming language that ships with Microsoft Access.

Launching Microsoft Access

You starts Microsoft Access like any of the usual windows applications. The most common way consists of clicking Start -> Programs -> Microsoft Access. As a member of the Microsoft Office suite, you can start the application by clicking Start -
> New Office Document. You can also create a shortcut on your desktop.Then, you can start creating your database.

Microsoft Access allows you to create a database from one of two processes: from scratch or by using one of the templates. However you start, you can add objects or fields almost as if you were switching from one techni☐ue to another.

Microsoft Access is e☐uipped with wizards, everywhere, some of which are not even installed by default during program setup. Although wizards are mostly efficient,

you should know what they are doing because more than once you will want to customize a behavior they have configured. A classic example I know is that whenever you ask Microsoft Access to insert a US ZIP Code in a table, the field is configured for a 5+4 format; most of the times, you don't need the last four digits, so you have to delete them manually. I encourage you to use wizards as long as you know what they are doing. If you want more control, you might have to do (some) things manually.

Practical Learning: Starting Microsoft Access

1.   To start Microsoft Access, click Start->Programs -> MicrosoftAccess.

2. When Microsoft Access starts, you receive the first dialog. This dialog allows you to decide on what you are planning to do.

The first radio button allows you to create a database from scratch. The second will help you create a database from one of the available and installed templates/samples. If you already have a database file on your computer, floppy disk, on someone else's computer you have access to (through a network), use the third radio button to locate it.

For this lesson, click the Open An Existing File radio button.

3. Locate the VBAccess Exercises folder where you installed the exercises for this tutorial. Then locate the VBAccess Exercises folder

4. Click the **Grier Summer Camp1** database and click Open.

Presenting Microsoft Access

Microsoft Access shares part of the look of Microsoft Office applications.

On top of the application, you see a long bar. On it left is the System icon with the usual key symbol. On the right side of the title bar, you see the windows system buttons that allow you to minimize, maximize, restore, or close the application.

Under the title bar is the Menu Bar with words like File, Edit, View, etc.

Under the menu is the toolbar. Toolbars change more regularly here than on most classic Microsoft Office applications. For example, the current toolbar is called the Form View toolbar. If you touch almost any object on your interface, a new toolbar comes up (you will have fun with them).

The most usual object of the interface is the Database Window.

- To access the Database Window, **press F11.**

The Database Window is made of different parts.On its own title bar, you see the name of the current database.Under the title bar is the Database Window's toolbar, this one also changes a lot depending on the object selected.

On the left side of the Database, Microsoft Access Objects is listed by categories. Once you click a category, objects of that category display on the right, wide section of the Database Window.

Tables

To do its work, Microsoft Access organizes a database into objects that we should get familiar with.

1.   On the Database Window, clickTables.

In the right section, double-click tblEmployees. The tblEmployees table opens.

2.   After viewing the table, to close it, click the close button on its top right corner

Queries

Although looking like a table, a query is a question you ask the database about available data, and the computer responds by display appropriate results. When creating a query, you tell the database what data you are concerned with and what categories you want the database to isolate. You can use a query to define new fields based on existing ones. Therefore, there are various kinds of queries.

You create a query by defining criteria, then Microsoft Access examines available data, if it finds data that matches your criteria, it shows you the result.

From our database, we are going to create a query where we will ask the database to provide a list of employees that includes only the employee number, the last name, title, and the office location.

1. To open a query, click the Queries button.

2. Double-click **dry Members By T-shirt Size**

3. After viewing the query, to close it, click its Close button.

Forms

A form is a user friendly interface you provide to your user(s) for easier data entry. Depending on your creative and artistic ability, a form's interface is usually better looking that anything else in your database.

To create a form, you first decide where its data will come from. Since we have already seen that data in a database resided on tables, data on a form first originates from a table, it could also come from a query, from more than one table or various queries. Data on a form can also be made of calculated or combined fields. All these could be done from known fields or from programmatically created fields.

During design, you should make sure you get a fairly good looking form by using appropriate font, sizes, colors and special styles. Most of these features can also be controlled programmatically where you will ask the computer to assign particular settings such as colors, etc when a certain condition is met.

1. To see a form, click the Forms button.
2. Double-click frmCamps.

3. After viewing the form, close it.

Reports

A report is the desired form of data you want to print. In other words, it is a way of telling the computer, "Based on available data, this is what I would like you to print, and this is how I want it printed.

When creating a report, you have to be a little artistic because your business might depend on it. During design, you can specify font, color, size and other special items or features. When programming, you can ask the computer to make some decisions and print conditionally on some criteria you set. For example, you can ask the computer to print student grades in grades in red if these grades are below a set minimum. The computer can also be directed to automatically print account statements on a particular date of the month, once the system calendar shows the date and time, the computer will print and get the bank statement ready for shipping.

1. To view a report, click the Reports button under Objects.

2. Double-click rptCamps

3. After viewing the **report**, close it.

Data Access Pages

New to Microsoft Access 2000, Data Access Pages allow you to publish your information on the Internet or on an Intranet, and then share data with others.

So far, I have not seen any advantage of Data Access Pages. Therefore, for this tutorial, we will not learn and will not use them. If you want to publish your database to the Internet or to an intranet, I suggest you use ASP (Active Server Pages) or aspx.

Macros

New to Microsoft Access 2000, Data Access Pages allow you to publish your information on the Internet or on an Intranet, and then share data with others.

So far, I have not seen any advantage of Data Access Pages. Therefore, for this tutorial, we will not learn and will not use them. If you want to publish your database to the Internet or to an intranet, I suggest you use ASP (Active Server Pages) or aspx.

Modules

Modules are pieces of Visual Basic code that you use during programming to tell the computer what to do when, how, and using what.

1. To take a look at a module, click the Modules button in the Objects list.
2. Double-click modUtilities
3. View the code when Visual Basic launches.

Introduction to Microsoft Visual Basic

Visual Basic is the most widely used programming language for creating Windows applications. Why? Because it's easy to learn, and doesn't require you to memorize difficult commands like other programming languages. In this course, you'll learn how to write Windows applications and programs using the Visual Basic programming language and the Visual Basic development environment.

Creating a Windows application ordinarily requires you to write lengthy and complex code. But, as you'll see, the Visual Basic development environment relieves you of this task. Instead, it enables you to create the application program and its components literally with the click of a button or menu item. It even writes all of the necessary code to get the application started for you, which you can then view and fine-tune.

Although I am using both MS Access 97 and MS Access 2000 for this tutorial, the following description is given for MS Access 2000. Although the following description and screenshots are given for MS Access 2000, if you are using MS Access 97, don't worry and simply ignore it. You don't need to upgrade.

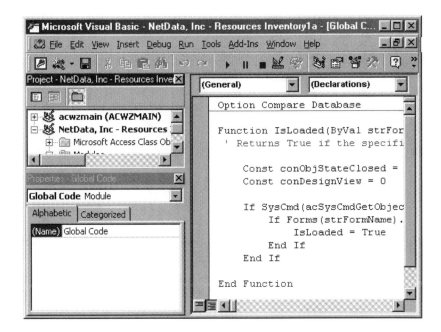

To ke most toolbars you are familiar with, to know what a particular button is used for, position your mouse on top and view a tooltip.

Almost any section of Visual Basic is dockable, which means it can be moved on the screen to another location.

The Project Explorer displays the coding objects available for your database. This window object is usually on the left of the window. To move it, click on its blue bar under the Standard toolbar and hold your mouse while you are dragging to the desired location. To position it back to its previous location, double-click its titlebar.

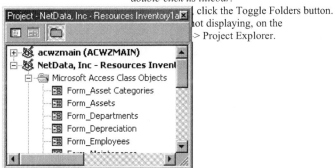

click the Toggle Folders button.
ot displaying, on the
> Project Explorer.

Every object and item of your database has properties associated with it. You control that properties when you design the object; for example, when you are designing a form in Microsoft Access, you define what its caption will be. You can as well have access to these properties in Microsoft Visual Basic. These properties are displayed in the Properties Window when the object is selected.

Since the Project Explorer and the Properties Window usually share the same section of the window (it is better that way), you can shrink one and heighten the other. To do that, position the mouse on the gray bar between both window.When the mouse pointer turns into a short line with a double arrow, click and drag.

The Code window is the area where you will mostly be working, this is largest section of the studio. It is mainly made of three sections.

On top, there are two combo boxes. The Object combo box allows you to select a particular object and access its events, actions that the object can launch. The Procedure combo box allows you to select a action, related to the object in the Object combo box, that you want to control.

The big and wide area is where you will be writing code. There are one vertical and one horizontal scroll bars that allow you to move left and right, up and down in case your code is using more space than the code window can display.

There are two small button on the left side of the horizontal scroll bar. The Full Module View button is used to display the whole associated with an object. The Procedure View button will display only the public procedures associated with the database.

Closing Microsoft Access and Visual Basic

The version of Microsoft Visual Basic we are using here is "For Applications".Indeed, you can create a fairly functional application with this version, but it is related to Microsoft Access (or Microsoft Office). To launch it, you should be in Microsoft Access. On the main menu (of any Microsoft Office application), you would click Tools -> Macro -> Visual Basic Editor.

When you are in the editor window of Microsoft Visual Basic, you can get back to Microsoft Access either from the View Microsoft Access button on the Standard toolbar, or by clicking a Microsoft Access object on the Taskbar. The shortcut to get back to Microsoft Access is Alt + F11.

You can close Microsoft Visual Basic any time and keep Microsoft Access running. If you close Microsoft Access, Microsoft Visual Basic will be closed also.

1. On the Standard toolbar of Microsoft Visual Basic, click the View Microsoft Access button to get back to the database.

2. To close Microsoft Access, press Alt + F4.

Chapter two
Overview of Windows Events

Introduction to Message Boxes

In order for a user to interact with the machine, computer programmers equip their applications with objects called controls. Almost every type of object that displays a physical presence on your monitor screen is referred to as a control as defined on this site.

The most fundamental control in the world of Visual Basic is a form. A form is rectangular object that is used to hold other controls. These other controls cannot exist by themselves: they need a host or parent, which is the role of the form.

The most commonly used form or dialog box is called a message box. It is used to display a message to the user who must click a button on the message box in order to close the dialog box. A message box looks as follows:

MsgBox "*Message To Display*"
The word MsgBox, which stands for Message Box, is required. The message to display can be typed inside of double-quotes. At this time, that form of the simplest message box is the one we will be using until we learn more details about message boxes.

Practical Learning: Using a Form

1. Start Microsoft Access. On the opening dialog box, click the first radio button to create a blank database and click OK
2. Change the file name to **Fundamentals** and click Create
3. On the main menu, click Insert -> Form
4. On the New Form dialog box, click Design View and click OK
5. To save the form, on the Form Design toolbar, click the Save button.
6. Type **frmMain** and press Enter

Introduction To Events

Microsoft Windows is a event-driven operating system. Whenever you do   something on the computer such as typing, moving or clicking the mouse, the application you are using, for example a word processor, a calculator, or a personal information manager (PIM), sends a message to the operating system, which is Microsoft Windows. The action of sending a message to the operating system is called a event. When an event is sent to the operating system, the object that sends the event is said to "fire" the event. Once the operating system has received a event, it analyses what you did, interprets it, and sends you the result to the   best of its interpretation. To be an effective database developer or programmer, you should be aware of events and how they work.

To use a program, you have to "Load" it into memory; the computer will do it for you. And to load a program, you have to select and start it. That's why you need to find it and...

When a program starts, it is said to be launched. Visual Basic considers that the program is Opening. It takes just an few seconds for a program to launch or open. After the program has been launched, it is said to be Loaded. Loading and running would mean the same thing, especially in Visual Basic.In reality, there are many events that the same control can send. To better manage the computer resources, the events are sent in sequence but one at a time.

These actions are events you create. There are other actions the computer performs behind the scenes, sometimes for its own maintenance. But, regardless, an event is an event. The beauty of Visual Basic programming is that you have to take care of only your initiated events, the computer takes care of itself.

Practical Learning: Launching, Loading, And Running a Program

1.   To start WordPad, click Start -> Programs -> Accessories ->WordPad.

2.   While the program is Opening, you should see a brief splash screen (since WordPad is a small application (not by programming standard, but as far as the users are concerned), the splash screen might not appear, or it would be very brief):

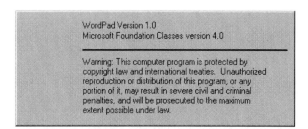

WordPad Version 1.0
Microsoft Foundation Classes version 4.0

Warning: This computer program is protected by
copyright law and international treaties. Unauthorized
reproduction or distribution of this program, or any
portion of it, may result in severe civil and criminal
penalties, and will be prosecuted to the maximum
extent possible under law.

3.   Notice that, after launching, WordPad is opened. Visual Basic considers that WordPad is Loaded:

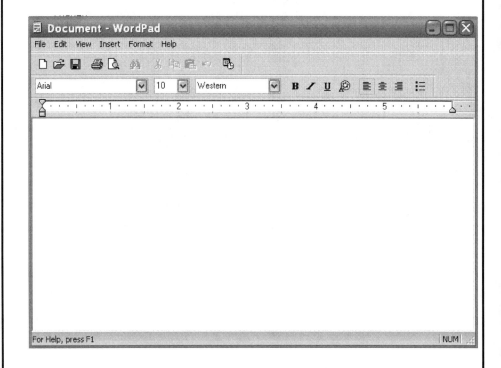

4.   Return to Microsoft Access

Event Proprietorship

A event is initiated by an entity; this could be the computer, an application, an form, a control, an report, a web page, or something else. The component that initiates the event needs to control its behavior. This allows other components to trust it to handle "its own business" so the others can expect a reliable result. To accomplish that, an event is considered a private matter.

Therefore, the coding of each event starts with the Private keyword. This is to let other components know that, "Let me handle this, OK? Trust me and just see what I can do." Not all actions are private, as we will learn. But at this time, we consider that an event starts with:

Private

A event is really an assignment you ask the application, the form, or the control to perform in response to a particular action happening. You can even ask a control perform an action based on the behavior of another control or based on the computer doing something (such as displaying 12:00 PM). The actions are called Procedures. There are two kind's of procedures: *Functions and Sub Procedures*.

Both are written in Visual Basic.

A Function is a general assignment you write in Visual Basic. This assignment is a resource for other events or actions to get results. For example, if many controls on a form would require a particular value or the result of a particular calculation, you can write a function that all desired events can refer to and get the appropriate result. Since other events and functions would expect a particular result from it, a function is expected to Return a value. And we will learn what kind of value this could be.

A Sub procedure is a type of assignment that applies to the an event associated with a particular database, form, report, or other control. It is used to "enclose" the coded assignment you want an event to carry. For example, if you want to display an message when an form loads, you would write the code of the Load event in a Sub Procedure. Since each event is a procedure, now we have:

Private Sub

Each object, such as an form, in your program has a name, and we will learn that each control (buttons, combo boxes, check boxes) has an name. Each form or each control has its own events. We will also see that different controls can have the same kind of event. You ought to let Visual Basic know whose action, I mean sub procedure, you are writing the event for. This is done by specifying its name.Here is a example:

Private Sub ControlName

There are many events associated with a form or a particular control. Therefore, we need to specify what particular event we are writing code for. The name of the event is written after the name of the control. To distinguish between a control's name and its event, Visual Basic uses a convention of displaying an underscore between them, like this:

Private Sub ControlName_Event

Since a sub procedure is an assignment and there could be various assignments in your program, such an event starts with Private Sub. Now, you should let Visual Basic know where an assignment ends. This is done with End Sub, like this:

Private Sub ControlName_Event End Sub

As mentioned already, and we will learn how a function returns a value, there are two important matters with the assignment a event is supposed to carry: the subject of the assignment and the necessary accessories to carry the assignment.

The subject of the assignment is called the body. It is written between the Private Sub and End Sub lines: this is where you specify what the event is supposed to accomplish. Some events just need to know what you want them to do, for   example, you can ask a button to close an form when that button is clicked. This   could be as simple as that.On the other hand, when the user clicks somewhere on a form, you could ask the form to display something.

Some events have or use just the body of the code to carry their assignment. Some other events will need some values from you. In some situations it will be one   value, in some others it could be more. The group of values that a event needs is called argument. Again, depending on the event, this could be one argument, or it could be as many as necessary.

The argument or group of arguments that the event might need would be listed in parentheses on the right side of the Event name, like this:

Private Sub ControlName_Event (Argument1, Argument2, Argumentn)
End Sub

Even if an event doesn't need a argument, you should provide empty parentheses, like this:

Private Sub ControlName_Event () End Sub

An form or a control has a usual event that it performs, if nothing else. The event is called the Default event.

Programming Events

There are various ways you can initiate an event on a control of your database application. In Microsoft Access, if you open an form or a report, you should access its Properties window. The events are usually stored on an form or a report.

Therefore, you should first open the form or the report whose event you want to program, in Design View. If the form or report "carries" the control whose event you want to program, you should also first open the form or report in Design View.

First Technique

1.   If you want to write code that relates to the whole form or event, double- click its selection button which is at the intersection of the rulers.

If you want to write code for a control, on the form or report, double-click the control to display its Properties window.

2.   Once the Properties window is displaying, you have a lot of alternatives. Click the Event property sheet and inspect the list of events:

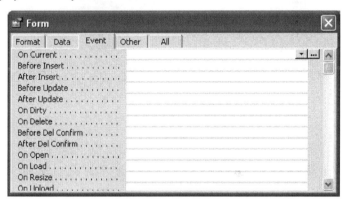

3.   After locating the event you want, double-click it. The [Event Procedure] clause will be added to the event. Once the [Event procedure] is displaying, click the ellipsis button ⊡to launch Microsoft Visual Basic. The keyboard caret would be positioned in the event and wait for you.

•   **Second Technique**

1.   On the Properties window, click the event to reveal its combo box.

2.   Click the arrow of the combo box and click [Event procedure].

3.   Once [Event Procedure] is displaying for an event, click the ellipsis button   of the event. This would launch Microsoft Visual Basic and would position the caret in the event's body,

waiting for your coding instructions.

- **Third Technique**

1.   Right-click the form, report or control whose event you want to write code for.

2.   Click Build Event...

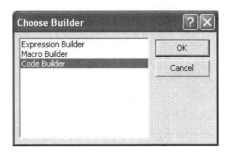

3.   On the Choose Builder dialog box, click Code Builder and click OK. This would launch Microsoft Visual Basic with the default event of the form, report, or control

- **Fourth Technique**

1.   As we saw earlier when reviewing the events, first open a form or report in Microsoft Access.

2.   To launch Microsoft Visual Basic, click the Code button in Microsoft Access.

3.   In the Object combo box, select the form (or report) to launch its default event.

4.   In the Procedure combo box, select the event you want.

Sometimes you or Microsoft Visual Basic will have inserted an event that you didn't want or that you don't want to program. If this happens, simply ignore the event: you do not have to delete it because if an event has been initiated but no code was written for it, Microsoft Visual Basic will take care of deleting it when you save the form or report.

Anatomy of an Event

The above introduction was meant to show you what a coded event looks like. Microsoft Visual Basic will do a lot of work for you behind the scenes. For example, it will always set a beginning and end event for you, reducing your headache. It will also specify the names (and types) of arguments for you.

Your programming will occur in Microsoft Visual Basic. Whenever the behavior you want to implement cannot be achieved in Microsoft Access, you will have to launch MS VB.

Practical Learning: Launching, Loading, And Running A Program

1. In Microsoft Access, make sure the from Main form is opened in Design View

2. On the Database toolbar, click the Code button

3. Notice that the Code Editor displays

4. Type:

Private Sub Form_Load

5. Press Enter.

6. Notice that Visual Basic added the parentheses and the *End Sub* line.

7. AlsonoticethatthecursorispositionedbetweenthePrivatelineandtheEndSubline.

Form's Events

Every Windows control you will use in your application has a set of events it can fire to carry its assignments. This is also valid for a form. Some of the events, as you   will see, are appropriate for a particular control or an action performed on the database. Some and many other events are shared by various controls.

Nevertheless, as a host for other controls, a form has specific events it can fire.

The Open Event

The On Open event is the first event a form fires when it is opened or when it is switched from Design View to Form View. You can use this event to perform some checking on the form or its controls while the form is opening but before it formally displays to the user

The Load Event

After the form opens, it installs itself in the computer memory. When installing itself, the form fires an On Load event. This is the favorite event you can use to perform any action or operation at startup. This event fires before the user can do anything but when the operating system is aware of the form. Once the form has been loaded, it become a regular control but can still manage the presence of other controls on it.

The Resize Event

For the operating system to be aware of a form as a Windows control, the form needs to be drawn on the screen (the monitor). This is because the operating needs to know the dimensions of the form. Whenever the dimensions of the form are set   or reset, an event called On Resize is sent to the operating system.

The Un Load Event

After using the form, if you close it, the memory that the form was used must be emptied and all cleaning related to other controls hosted by the form must take place. To take care of this, an event called On Un Load is sent to the operating system. This is the opposite event to the On Load.

The Close Event

After the form has been removed from the screen, that is, once the form has been closed, an On Close event fires.

Practical Learning: Using Form's Events

1.   Type:

Private Sub Form Load ()

MsgBox "The form has been loaded" End

Sub

2.   Return to Microsoft Access and switch the form to Form View. Notice that a message box displays

3.   Return to the Code Editor or Visual Basic. Notice that the Object combo box is displaying the word Form.

4.   Click the arrow of the Object combo box to display its list.

The Object combo box displays a list including the form and its controls, if any is positioned on the form.

5.   Notice that the Procedure combo box is displaying Load.

6.   Click the arrow of the Procedure combo box to display the events of the form:

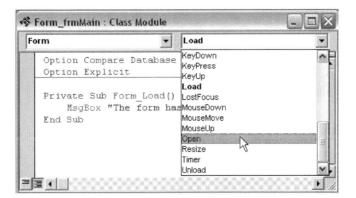

7.   Click Open

8.   Change the code of the event as follows:

Private Sub Form Open (Cancel As Integer) MsgBox

"The form is not opened"

End Sub

9.   Switch to Microsoft Access.

10.   Notice that the message box for the Open event displays first. After you click OK, the message box for the Load event displays. This indicates that the Open event takes precedence over the Load event.

Fundamental Events: Click

To interact with the computer, one of the most usually actions the user performs is to click the mouse. The mouse is equipped with two buttons. The most clicked button is the left one.

Because the action simply consists of clicking, when the user presses this button, a simple event, called Click is sent or fired. When the user presses the (left) button on the mouse, the mouse pointer is usually on a Windows control. Based on this, the control that is clicked "owns" the event and must manage it. Therefore, no detailed information is provided as part of the event. The operating system believes that the control that fired the event knows what to do and should take care of everything.

For this reason, whenever you decide to code an On Click event, you should make sure you know what control sent or fired the event. This is (one of) the most common events of Windows controls.

Practical Learning: Firing an OnClick Event

1.   To see what the On Click event looks like, on the Object combo box, select Detail.

2.   Notice that the skeleton for the Click event of the Detail section of the form is displaying.AlsonoticetheOnClickeventdoesnotcarrymuchinformation.

3.   Implement the event as follows:

Private Sub Detail Click ()
MsgBox "The form has been clicked" End
Sub

4.   Switch back to Microsoft Access. Switch the form to Form View and click in the middle of the form to see a message box.

5.   Switch the form back to Design View

Fundamental Events: The Double-Click Event

To make the mouse more useful and to verify its role, another action can be performed on it. This consists of pressing the left button very fast twice. This action initiates an event known as On DblClick.

By default, the DblClick event provides a simple structure to the programmer. You must know what control has been double-clicked and what you want to do. This means that the operating system relies on the control that "owns" the event.

Practical Learning: Firing an On DblClick Event

1.   While Detail is still selected in the Object combo box, in the Procedure combo box, select DblClick

2.   Notice the structure of the event

3.   Remove or delete the MsgBox line of the Detail Click event and implement the Detail_DblClick event as follows:

Private Sub Detail_DblClick (Cancel As Integer) MsgBox "The form
has been double-clicked"
End Sub

4.   Switch to Microsoft Access and switch the form to Form View

5.   Double-click in the middle of the form

6.   After reading the message box, clicking OK

7.   Switch to the Code Editor and delete all events or at least their contents (between the Private and End Sublines)

Fundamentals of Coding: The Indentation

Indentation if a technique that allows you to write easily readable code. It consists of visually showing the beginning and end of an event (or procedure, as we will learn). Indentation consists of moving your code to the right side so that the only line to the extreme left are those of the Private and End Sublines.

The easiest and most common way to apply indentation consists of pressing Tab before typing your code. By default, one indentation, done when pressing Tab, corresponds to 4 characters. This is controlled by the Module property sheet of the Options dialog box. To change it, on the main menu of Microsoft Access 97, click Tools -> Options and click the Module tab:

If you are using Microsoft Access 2000 or 2002, or on the main menu of Visual Basic, click Tools -> Options and click the Editor Property sheet.

If you don't want the pressing of Tab to be equivalent to 4 characters, change the value of the Tab

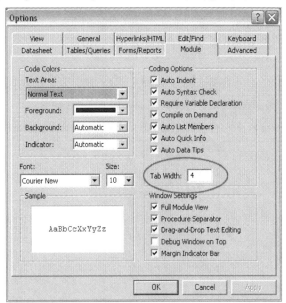

Width text box to a reasonable integer value and click OK. Otherwise, it is (strongly) suggested that you keep to its default of 4 characters.

Practical Learning: Firing an On DblClick Event

1.   Click anywhere on the line that has MsgBox and press Home

2.   Press Tab to change the Detail_DblClick event as follows:

Private Sub Detail_DblClick(Cancel As Integer) MsgBox "The form
has been double-clicked"
End Sub

3.   Save the form and close Microsoft Access.

Introduction to Controls Events

The controls used on Microsoft Windows's applications provide the main means of interaction with the computer. To make such interaction effective, they send regular message to the operating system. There are many controls and they send various messages. Although you might have seen a great quantity of controls on some other applications or programming environments, Microsoft Access by default presents all of the regular control that a database would need. When designing your database application, you will select which ever control applies to the result you are trying to achieve. Whenever you decide to use a particular control, you should know its characteristics and limitations, the events it can send and what those events do.

Practical Learning: Starting the Application

1.   Start Microsoft Access and open the **Fundamentals** application created in the previous lesson

2.   Open the **from Main** form. After viewing the form, close it.

Activating a Form

A regular database application is equipped with various forms that carry appropriate data. Each form is usually linked to a particular table. Since an application can have various forms, the user sometimes needs to open many of them at the same time, to view data from different forms.

Although a user can have two or more forms on screen at the same time, the user can perform any direct operation on only one form.

When two forms are present on the screen, only one of the forms can receive input from the user. The title bar of such a form displays a different color than the title bar of the other. In the following picture, compare the colors on the title bars of the Find and the Date and Time dialog boxes:

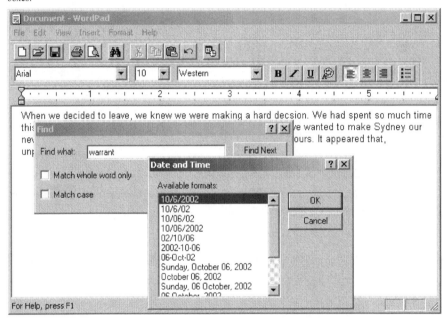

In Microsoft Access, the form that can receive input from the user is said to be active. If you want to use the other form (s), you must first make them active. To indicate the form that is active, Microsoft Access refers to the Control Panel where the Display manages colors for the applications. The color of the title bar of the active form is set by the Active Title Bar color of the Appearance property sheet.

When an application has two forms. The form that is active is, in Cartesian coordinates, above the other forms. If you click a area of another form (provided the forms are modeless or a child of the application) the other form becomes active. If you close the active form, the form that was second in Cartesian coordinates becomes active. Whenever a form becomes active, to make its presence or "activeness" be known to the operating system, the form sends an OnActive event to the operating system. If another form becomes active, the form that was active sends an On DeActive event to the operating system, letting it know that it has lost that privilege.

Practical Learning: Making a Form Active

1.   To create a new form, in the Forms section of the Database Window, click New

2.   Make sure Design View is selected and click OK.

3.   Save the form as *from Second* and switch it to Design View if necessary

4.   On the Form Design toolbar, click the Code button

5.   Verify that the title bar of the Code Editor displays Form from Second. In the Object combo box, select Form.

6.   In the Procedure combo box, select Active

7.   Press Tab and implement the event as follows:

Private Sub Form Activate()

MsgBox "Second in Command: I am in Active duty now" End Sub

8.   Return to Microsoft Access and switch the **from Second** form to Form View. Notice that a message box displays

9.   Click OK to close the message box but leave the from Second form open.

10.   On the Database Window, double-click the from Main form to open it.

11.   In the background, click the other form to make it active. Notice that the message box displays again. Click OK

Chapter Three
Overview of Events: The Focus Events

Microsoft Windows operating systems allow the user of your database to work on more that one form at the same time. In fact, they allow the user to work on as many forms as the computer can handle. But only one form can receive instructions at a given time. As we saw in the last exercise, only one form can be active at a time. When a form becomes active, we consider that it has received focus.

Just as an application can have many forms, a form can be e□uipped with various controls. Such is the case for any data entry form. On an form that is e□uipped with many controls, only one control can be changed at a time; such a control is said to have focus. As we saw that the form that has focus usually has its title bar with the active window color as set in Control Panel, in an form with many controls, the one that has focus will usually have a cursor or a dotted line around its selection.

When an form or a control has focus, Microsoft Visual Basic applies the Got Focus event to that form or control. If the focus shifts to another form or control, the control that had focus fires an Lost Focus event and sends it to the operating system.

Practical Learning: Using an OnFocus Event

1.   Get back to the Code Editor.
To see the structure of an On Got Focus event, on the Procedure combo box, select Got Focus

2.   Press Tab and implement the event as follows:

Private Sub Form Got Focus ()
MsgBox "I am the focus of attention now. Give it to me" End Sub

3.   Notice that the On Got Focus has a structure similar to the On Click event. Get
back to Microsoft Access and click the from Second form.

4.   Notice that the message box for the Active event comes up first. After you click OK, the

message box for the Got Focus event displays.

5.   Click OK.

Consequently, note that the Active event fires before the Got Focus event.

6.   Get back to Microsoft Access and close the from Second form.

7.   When asked whether you want to save the changes, click No.

8.   Switch the from Main form to Design View.

If the Properties window is not displaying, double click the inside the form. If the Tool box
is not displaying, on the Form Design toolbar, click Toolbox

9.   On the Toolbox, click Text Box and click on the form. Change the label to First Name: and,
using the Properties window, change the name of the text box to txt First Name

10.   Add another text box to the form. Change its label to Last Name: and change the name of
the text box to txt Last Name

11.   Access the Code Editor.

12.   In the Object combo box, click txt First Name

13.   In the Procedure combo box, select Got Focus

14.   Press Tab and implement it as follows:

Private Sub txt First Name Got Focus () txt First Name =
"I have focus"
End Sub

15.   In the Procedure com box, select Lost Focus and implement it as follows:

Private Sub txt First Name Lost Focus () txt First Name
= "I lost it!!!"
End Sub

16. Return to Microsoft Access. In the from Main form, click in the First Name text box. Notice the sentence that displays in it.

17. Press Tab to move the cursor away. Notice that the First Name text box displays another message

Giving Focus

As you have seen, only one form among other form can be active for the user. On a form that has many controls, only one control can receive input from the user. Two problems will regularly happen to your users while they are performing data entry: they need to have the right form or control and they need to make sure they are entering data in the intended control. At all times, it is certainly your responsibility to make these items accessible. With code, you can specify which control has focus and when. This can tremendously make the users' job easier.

To give focus to a control when another action happens, type the name of the control followed by the period operator, followed by the Set Focus procedure. An example would be:

Private Sub txt First Name Got Focus () txt Address. Set Focus
End Sub

Keyboard Events

Word processing consists of manipulating text and characters on your computer until you get the fantastic result you long for. To display these characters, you press some keys on your keyboard.If the application is configured to receive text, your pressing actions will display characters on the screen.

The keyboard is also used to perform various other actions such as accepting what a dialog box displays or dismissing it. When the user presses the keys on a keyboard, The control in which the characters are being typed to sends one or more messages to the operating system.

There are three main events that Microsoft Windows associates to the keyboard.

• **OnKeyDown:** When the user presses a key on the keyboard, an event called KeyDown is sent to the operating system.

• **OnKeyUp:** When you release a key that was pressed, a even called KeyUp is sent to the operating system. These last two events apply to almost any key on your keyboard, even if the user is not typing; that is, even if the result of pressing a key did not display a character on the document.

• **OnKeyPress:** The KeyPress event is sent if the key the user pressed is recognized as a character key; that is, a key that would result in displaying a character in a document.

When programming your database, you will need to know what result you are expecting, then choose the right event. Some keys on the keyboard do not display anything on a document. Instead, they perform (only) an action. Examples of such keys are Enter, Tab, Esc. Therefore, if you mean to find out what key the user pressed, use the OnKeyDown event and not the OnKeyPress event, even though the user will have pressed a key.

Practical Learning: Keyboard Events

1.   To see the list of keyboard events and their structures, click the arrow of the Procedure combo box and selectKeyDown.

2.   Notice the structure of the event:

Private Sub txtFirstName_KeyDown(KeyCode As Integer, Shift As Integer) End Sub

3.   To call another keyboard event, on the Procedure combo box, select OnKeyPress:

Private Sub txtFirstName_KeyPress(KeyAscii As Integer) End Sub

4.   In the Procedure combo box, select KeyUp and notice its event:

Private Sub txtFirstName_KeyUp(KeyCode As Integer, Shift As Integer) End Sub

Mouse Events: The MouseDown

A mouse is equipped with buttons, usually two, that the user presses to request an action. Compared to the keyboard, the mouse claims many more events that are directly or indirectly related to pressing one of its buttons.

When the user presses one of the buttons on the mouse, an event, called OnMouseDown, is sent to the operating system. This event carries enough information for the programmer as three arguments. It is your responsibility to let the operating know what to do:

Private Sub txtFirstName_MouseDown(Button As Integer, Shift As Integer, X As Single, Y AsSingle)

End Sub

- The operating system needs to know what button was pressed; this is represented as the left or the right button. The left button is known as **vbLeftButton**. The right button is referenced as **vbRightButton**. If the mouse is equipped with a middle button, it would **vbMiddleButton**. In reality, these buttons have (constant) numeric values of 0, 1, and 2respectively.

- Secondly, the operating system needs to know whether a special key, Shift, Ctrl, or Alt, was pressed. These buttons are called **vbShiftMask**, **vbCtrlMask**, and **vbAltMask** respectively. In reality, they are represented with 1, 2, and 4 respectively.

- Lastly, the operating system needs to know the screen coordinates of the mouse pointer, that is, the coordinates of the point where the mouse landed. X represents the distance from the top left corner of the screen to the right direction. Y represents the vertical measure of the point from the top-left corner down.

Mouse Events: The MouseUp

When the user releases a button that was pressed on the mouse, a new event is sent to the operating system. This event is called MouseUp. It provides the same types of information as the MouseDown event:

Private Sub txtFirstName_MouseUp(Button As Integer, Shift As Integer, X As Single, Y AsSingle)

End Sub

Mouse Events: The MouseMove

The MouseMove event is sent while the user is moving the mouse on the screen. It provides the same pieces of information as the MouseDown and the MouseUp events:

Private Sub txtFirstName_MouseMove (Button As Integer, Shift As Integer, X As Single, Y AsSingle)

End Sub

Practical Learning: The OnMouseDown and MouseUp Events

1.   Click the arrow of the Procedure combo box and selectMouseDown

2.   Notice the structure of the OnMouseDownevent.

3.   To initiate an OnMouseUp event, on the Procedure combo box, selectMouseUp.

4.   Close MicrosoftAccess

CHAPTER FOUR
Fields, Data Types, and Variables

Introduction

Data entry on a database is performed on forms. As far as users are concerned, forms are the most important parts of a database. For a database developer, data is in fact stored in tables. Therefore, as a database developer, you should/must primarily know how tables function.

Table Design

Visually, a table is made of cells. A cell on a table is simply the intersection of a column and a row:

	Employee ID	Empl #	Date Hired	Title	First Name	MI
⊞	1	65-4386	9/26/1992	Mrs	Laurentine	D
⊞	2	35-7690	12/30/1994	Mr	Jeremiah	
⊞	3	48-9349	4/14/1995	Ms	Monique	P
⊞	4	34-2908	10/5/1996	Mrs	Christine	H
*	(AutoNumber)					

tblEmployees : Table — Record: 1 of 4

A column is a category of information. All data on a particular table conforms to the exact same kind of data. This means that data on a particular column can be made of text. Data on another column can be configured for numeric values. Another column can restrict the type of data that is entered on its fields.

This analysis shows us that a column in fact controls data that is entered on a table. To manage data entered under a column, Microsoft Access provides categories that control what type of data can, should, or must be entered in a cell. To specify a particular data type for a column, you must design the table that would hold the data. This is done in a special display of the table called Design View.

To display a table in Design View if you are just designing the table, from the New Table dialog box, click Design View. If you are using Microsoft Access 2000 or 2002, you can double-click Create Table in Design View.

Microsoft Access and VisualBasic Operators

Introduction

A expression is a combination of values and symbols that allows you to get an new value; such an new value can be used in another expression, it can also be made available to a procedure, or it can be displayed in a control. For example, to get a sum of two numbers that the user is supposed to enter in an form, when creating such a form or report, you would not know what the user entered in two boxes, but you can write a expression that would use whatever the user enters, to get an new value. The values involved in an expression could be external to the program, such as algebraic numbers; they could also come from the program itself, such as a BillingRate or a DateHired fields; and they could be a combination of algebraic numbers and controls content on your program.

Comments

In the programming world, a comment is a piece of text in Visual Basic code that Visual Basic (in reality the compiler) would not consider when reading your code. As such a comment can be written any way you want.

In Visual Basic, the line that contains a comment can start with a single quote. Here is an example: *Private Sub Form_Load ()*

'This line will not be considered as part of the code

End Sub

Alternatively, you can start a comment with the **Rem** keyword. Anything on the right side of rem, Rem, or REM would not be read. Here is an example:

Private Sub Form_Load ()

'This line will not be considered as part of the code

Rem I can write anything I want on this line

End Sub

Comments are very useful and you are strongly suggested to use comments regularly. They can never hurt your code and they don't increase the size of your application. Comments can help you and other people who read your code to figure out what a particular section of code is used for, which can be helpful when you re- visit your code after months or years of not seeing it.

The Assignment Operator =

The assignment operation is used to make a copy of a value, an expression, or the content of a control and give the copy to another field or expression. The assignment operation is performed with the = sign.

For example, suppose you have a field that displays a first name and that field is called FirstName. If you want that first name to display in another field, with this new field named, in the new field you could type:

=FirstName

On the other hand, you can use the assignment operator to give a value to a declared variable. Here is an example:

Private Sub Form_Load ()
Dim Number Of Tracks as Integer
Number Of Tracks = 16
End Sub

When the assignment operator is provided to a variable as a starting value for the variable, this is referred to as initializing the variable.

Practical Learning: Using the Assignment Operator

1. Open the **VBAccess1**application

2. Open the **Assignment**form

3. After viewing the form, switch it to DesignView

4. On the form, click the First Name text box to selectit.

5. On the Properties window, click the Eventtab.

6. Double-click On LostFocus

7. Right-click On Lost Focus and clickBuild...

8. Implement the event asfollows:

Private Sub txtFirstName_Lost Focus ()
'Assign the content of the First Name textbox ' to the Full Name text

box

Txt Full Name = txtFirstName End Sub

9. Return to the form and switch it to FormView

10. Click the First Name text box. Type Catherine and pressTab

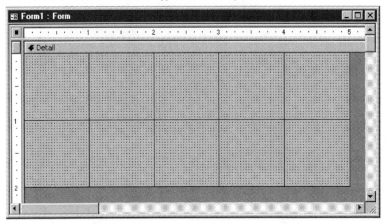

11. NoticethattheFullNametextboxgotfilledwiththevalueoftheFirstName   when   the
First Name text box lostfocus.

After using the form, switch it to Design View

The Double Quotes: ""

Double-quotes are used to display a string. First...

Astringisanemptyspace, a character, or agroup of characters that you type or provide to a
control and you want this character or this group of characters to be considered "as is". In
other words, the expression or the control that receives the string should keep it or them
the way you supplied it orthem.

A string can be an empty space or one character, such as $ or w; a group of characters, like
home or Manchester United or Verbally speaking, I mean… Ah forget it. Most of the time,
you will want the program to keep this character or group of characters exactly the way you or

the user supplied them. In order to let the program know that this is a string, you must enclose it in double quotes. From our examples, our strings would be "$", "w", "home", "Manchester United", and "Verbally speaking, I mean... Ah forget it".

To assign a string to an expression or a field, use the assignment operator as follows:

= "Manchester United"

In the same way, to initialize a variable with a string, use the assignment operator. Here is an example:

```
Private          Sub
Form_Load ()  Dim
Address As String
Address = "12404  Lockwood  Drive  AptD4"
End Sub
```

Practical Learning: Using the Double-Quote Operator

1.   On the Assign form, right-click the Full Name text box and click BuildEvent...

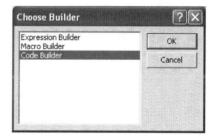

2.   On the Choose Builder dialog box, click Code Builder and clickOK

3.   OnceintheCodeEditor,intheObjectcombobox,selectcmdResetand implement its Click event asfollows:

```
Private Sub cmdReset_Click ()
'Make all text boxes empty
txtFirstName = "" txtMI
```

= "" txtLastName = ""
txtFullName   =   ""
txtUsername = ""
End Sub

4.   ClicktheemptylinebetweenPrivateSubtxtFullName_BeforeUpdateandEnd   Sub.
Notice that the Object combo box displaystxtFullName.

5.   IntheProcedurecombobox,selectDblClickandimplementtheeventas follows:

Private Sub txtFullName_DblClick(Cancel As Integer)
Dim strFullName As String strFullName =
"Mary   D.Lunden"   txtFullName   =
strFullName
End Sub

6.   Return to the form and double-click the Full Name textbox

The String Concatenator: &

The &operator is used to append two strings, the contents of two controls, or expressions;
this is considered as concatenating them. For example, it could allow you to concatenate a
first name and the last name, producing a full name.

The general syntax of the concatenation operator is expressed as:

Value1 &Value2

To display a concatenated expression, use the assignment operator on the field. To assign a
concatenated expression to a variable, use the assignment operator the same way:

Private Sub Form_Load ()
Dim FirstName, LastName AsString
Dim FullName AsString

FirstName   =
"Francis" LastName
="Pottelson"
FullName = FirstName & LastName

Text0   =
FullName End
Sub

To concatenate more than two expressions, you can use as many & operators between
any two expressions as necessary.

After concatenating the expressions or values, you can assign the result to another value or
expression using the assignment operator. The syntax used is:

=Field1 & " " & Field2

Examples

=FirstName & " " &LastName
This would display, for example, Boniface Dunkirk
= [LastName] & ", " & [FirstName]
This would produce, for example, Chang, Helene
= [Address] & " " & [City] & " " & [State] & " " &
[ZIPCode] & " " & [Country]
This would display a complete address in a field

Practical Learning: Using the Concatenator

1.   In the Code Editor, delete the code in the **txtFirstName_LostFocus**event

2.   IntheObjectcombobox,select**cmdCreateAccount**andimplementitsClickeventas follows:

```
Private  SubcmdCreateAccount_Click () Dim
strFirstName As String
Dim     strMiddleInitial    AsString    Dim
strLastName AsString
Dim  strFullName  AsString  Dim
strUsername AsString

StrFirstName =txtFirstName strMiddleInitial =
txtMI strLastName =txtLastName
                '                    Createausernamemadeofthelastnamefollowedbythemiddleinitial strUsername =
                                                    txtLastName &strMiddleInitial
```

' Createafullnameasthefirstnamefollowedbythelastname strFullName =
txtFirstName & " " &txtLastName

TxtFullName = strFullName txtUsername =
strUsername
End Sub

3. Return to the form and click FirstName

4. Type Hermine and pressTab

5. Type D and pressTab

6. In the Last Name text box, type Summers and pressTab

7. Notice that the first button is selected. PressEnter

8. Close the dialog box. When asked whether you want to save the form, clickYes.

The Negation Operator -

In mathematics, an integer such as 120 or a double floating number such as 98.005 is ualified as positive; that is, it is considered greater than 0. If a number is less than 0, to express it, you can add the - sign on the left side of the number.

Examples are -5502 or -240.65. The - sign signifies that the number is negative.

A variable or a expression can also be represented as negative by prefixing it with a - sign. Examples are - Distance or -NbrOfPlayers.

To display an negative value or a negative expression in a field, use the assignment operator. Here are examples:
= -95.12

= -Temperature

To initialize a variable with a negative value, use the assignment operator. Here is an example:

Private Sub Form_Load ()
Dim NumberOfTracks As Byte Dim Temperature As Integer
NumberOfTracks = 16
Temperature = -94
End Sub

The Addition: +

The addition is used to add one value or expression to another. It is performed using the + symbol and its syntax is:

Value1 + Value2

The addition allows you to add two numbers such as 12 + 548 or 5004.25 + 7.63

After performing the addition, you get an result. You can provide such an result to another variable or control. This is done using the assignment operator. The syntax used would be:

= Value1 + Value2

Practical Learning: Using the Addition

1. Open the frmAlgebraicOperators form.

2. After viewing it, switch it to Design View

3. The accompanying resources include pictures of geometric figures. To enhance the form, you can add them. To do that, on the Toolbox, click Image and click the left area of the labels. On the Insert Picture dialog box, locate the picture and add it.

4. On the form, click the Quadrilateral tab. Right-click the top Calculate button and click Build Event...

5. On the Choose Builder dialog box, double-click Code Builder.

6. In the Object combo box, select cmdRCalculate

7. Implement both Click events as follows:

```
Private Sub cmdRCalculate_Click()
Dim  dblLength,  dblHeight  AsDouble  Dim
dblPerimeter As Double

dblLength     =     txtRLength
dblHeight = txtRHeight
'                 Calculate the perimeter of therectangle
'                 by adding the length to the height, 2 times each
dblPerimeter=dblLength+dblHeight+dblLength+dblHeight txtRPerimeter
=dblPerimeter
End Sub

Private  SubcmdSqCalculate_Click()  Dim
dblSide As Double
Dim dblPerimeter As Double
```

```
dblSide = txtSqSide
'                    Calculatetheperimeterofasquarebyaddingtheside4times dblPerimeter =
dblSide + dblSide + dblSide +dblSide

txtSqPerimeter =dblPerimeter End Sub
```

1.   Return to the form and switch it to FormView

2.   In the Quadrilateral tab, click Side and type**35.55**

3.   Click the top **Calculate**button

4.   Click Length and type**42.72**

5.   Click Height and type**36.44**

6.   Click the other **Calculate**button

7.   After using the form, return to the CodeEditor

The Subtraction: -

The subtraction is performed by retrieving the one value from another value.This is done using the - symbol. The syntax used is:

Value1 - Value2

The value of Value1 is subtracted from the value of Value2. After the operation is performed, an new value results. This result can be used in any way you want. For example, you can display it in a control using the assignment operator as follows:

= Value1 - Value2

The Multiplication: *

The multiplication allows adding the one value to itself a certain number of times, set by the second value. The multiplication is performed with the * sign which is typed with Shift + 8. Here is an example:

Value1 * Value2

During the operation, Value1 is repeatedly added to itself, Value2 times. The result can be assigned to another value or displayed in a control as follows:

= Value1 * Value2

1.   To apply the multiplication operation, change the Click events asfollows:

```
Private Sub cmdRCalculate_Click()
Dim  dblLength,  dblHeight  AsDouble  Dim
dblPerimeter As Double
Dim dblArea As Double

dblLength      =      txtRLength
dblHeight = txtRHeight
'                 Calculate the perimeter of therectangle
'                 by adding the length to the height, 2 times each
dblPerimeter=dblLength+dblHeight+dblLength+dblHeight dblArea = dblLength
*dblHeight

txtRPerimeter  =  dblPerimeter  txtRArea  =
dblArea
End Sub


Private  SubcmdSqCalculate_Click()  Dim
dblSide AsDouble
Dim  dblPerimeter AsDouble  Dim
dblArea AsDouble

dblSide = txtSqSide
'                 Calculatetheperimeterofasquarebyaddingtheside4times dblPerimeter = 4
*dblSide
dblArea = dblSide * dblSide

txtSqPerimeter  =dblPerimeter  txtSqArea  =
dblArea
End Sub
```

2. Get back to the form and click both Calculatebuttons:

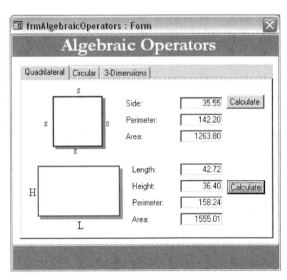

3. After using the form, switch it to Design View and get back to the CodeEditor

4. IntheObjectcombobox,select**cmdCCalculate**andimplementitsClickeventas follows:

```
Private     SubcmdCCalculate_Click()
Dim dblRadius As Double
Dim dblCircumference, dblArea As Double

dblRadius = txtCircleRadius
'                 Circumference of a circle = 2 * Radius *PI
dblCircumference = 2 * dblRadius *3.14159
'                 Area of a circle = Radius * Radius *PI
dblArea = 3.14159 * dblRadius *dblRadius

txtCircleCircumference =dblCircumference  txtCircleArea
= dblArea
End Sub
```

5. Return to the form and switch it to FormView

6. ClicktheCirculartabandchangethetopRadius(theradiusofthecircle)to64.88 and click the top Calculatebutton:

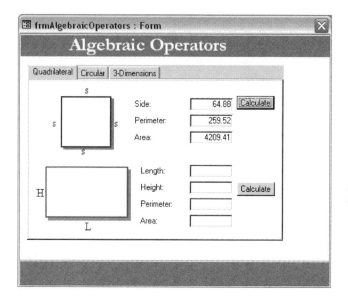

7. After using the form, switch it to DesignView

The Integer Division: \

Dividing an item means cutting it in pieces or fractions of a set value. For example, when you cut a apple in the middle, you are dividing it in 2 pieces. If you cut each one of the resulting pieces, you will get 4 pieces or fractions. This is considered that you have divided the apple in 4 divisions. Therefore, the division is used to get the fraction of one number in terms of another.

Microsoft Visual Basic provides two types of results for the division operation. If you want the result of the operation to be an natural number, called an integer, use the backlash operator "\" as the divisor. Here is an example:

Value1 \ Value2

This operation can be performed on two types of valid numbers, with or without decimal parts. After the operation, the result would be an natural number.

The result of the operation can be assigned to another value. It can also be displayed in a control using the assignment operator:

= Value1 \ Value2

The Division: /

The second type of division results in a decimal number. It is performed with the forward slash "/". Its syntax is:

Value1 / Value2

After the operation is performed, the result is a decimal number. The result of either operation can be assigned to another value. It can also be displayed in a control using the assignment operator:

= Value1 / Value2

The Exponentiation: ^

Exponentiation is the ability to raise a number to the power of another number. This operation is performed using the ^ operator (Shift + 6). It uses the following mathematical formula:

y^x

In Microsoft Visual Basic (and Microsoft Access), this formula is written as y^x and means the same thing. Either or both y and x can be values or expressions, but they must carry valid values that can be evaluated.

When the operation is performed, the value of y is raised to the power of x. You can display the result of such an operation in a field using the assignment operator as follows:

=y^x

You can also assign the operation to an expression as follows: Total

= y^x

Practical Learning: Using the Exponentiation Operator

1.   ReturntotheCodeEditorandchangethecodeofthecmdSqCalculate_Clickas follows:

Private   SubcmdSqCalculate_Click()   Dim
dblSide AsDouble

Dim dblPerimeter AsDouble Dim
dblArea AsDouble

dblSide = txtSqSide
' Calculate the perimeter of a square by adding the side 4 times dblPerimeter = 4 * dblSide
dblArea = **dblSide ^ 2**

txtSqPerimeter =dblPerimeter txtSqArea =
dblArea
End Sub

2.   Get to the form and switch it to FormView.

3.   IntheQuadrilateralpropertysheet,enter12.46intheSidetextboxandclickthe top**Calculate**

4.   After using the form, switch it to DesignView

The Remainder Operator: Mod

The division operation gives a result of a number with or without decimal values, which is fine in some circumstances. Sometimes you will want to get the value remaining after a division renders a natural result. Imagine you have 26 kids at a football (soccer) stadium and they are about to start. You know that you need 11 kids for each team to start. If the game starts with the right amount of players, how many will seat and wait? The remainder operation is performed with keyword Mod. Its syntax is:

Value1 Mod Value2

The result of the operation can be used as you see fit or you can display it in a control using the assignment operator as follows:

= Value1 Mod Value2

The Parentheses Operators: ()
Parentheses are used in two main circumstances: in a event (or procedures, as we will learn) or in an operation. The parentheses in an operation help to create sections in an operation. This regularly occurs when more than one operators are used in an operation.
Consider the following operation: 8 + 3 * 5

The result of this operation depends on whether you want to add 8 to 3 then multiply the result by 5 or you want to multiply 3 by 5 and then add the result to 8. Parentheses allow you to specify which operation should be performed first in a multi-operator operation. In our example, if you want to add 8 to 3 first and use the result to multiply it by 5, you would write (8 + 3) * 5. This would produce 55. On the other hand, if you want to multiply 3 by 5 first then add the result to 8, you would write 8 + (3 * 5). This would produce 23.

As you can see, results are different when parentheses are used on an operation that involves various operators. This concept is based on a theory called operator precedence. This theory manages which operation would execute before which one; but parentheses allow you to completely control the sequence of these operations.

Practical Learning: Using the Exponentiation Operator

1.   Get to the Code Editor and change the followingevent:

```
Private Sub cmdRCalculate_Click()
Dim  dblLength,  dblHeight  AsDouble  Dim
dblPerimeter As Double
Dim dblArea As Double

dblLength    =    txtRLength
dblHeight = txtRHeight
                                               '         Calculate the perimeter of therectangle
        '              by adding the length to the height, 2 timeseach
    dblPerimeter = 2 * (dblLength + dblHeight)dblArea = dblLength
                                        *dblHeight

txtRPerimeter  =  dblPerimeter  txtRArea  =
dblArea
End Sub
```

2.   In the Object combo box, select **cmdECalculate** and implement its event asfollows:

```
Private Sub cmdECalculate_Click()
Dim  dblRadius1,  dblRadius2  As  Double  Dim
dblCircumference, dblArea AsDouble

dblRadius1  =txtEllipseRadius1  dblRadius2
=txtEllipseRadius2
dblCircumference = (dblRadius1 + dblRadius2) * 3.14159
```

```
dblArea = dblRadius1 * dblRadius2 * 3.14159
```

```
txtEllipseCircumference =dblCircumference txtEllipseArea = dblArea
End Sub
```

3.   Return to the form. Test the rectangle and theellipse.

The S☐uare Brackets Operator: []

When reviewing name rules for our objects in Microsoft Access, we saw that we should use names that are made of one word (no space). In reality, Microsoft Access, as mentioned already, is particularly flexible with names. Therefore, it uses an mechanism to delimit an name when such an name is involved in an operation.

The operator used to specify the beginning of an name is the left or opening s☐uare bracket [. At the end of a name, a right or closing bracket is used. To be safe, whether a name is made of one or more words, Microsoft prefers including it in square brackets.

Therefore, in an operation, also called an expression, instead of using such an name as FirstName, you should use [FirstName]. Of course, if a name is made of more than one word, which is frequent on databases created using the Database Wizard, you must always include it in square brackets. A example would be [Video Titles Subform]

Practical Learning: Using the Square Brackets Operator

1.   Get to the Code Editor and change the followingevents:

```
Private Sub cmdRCalculate_Click()
Dim  dblLength,  dblHeight  AsDouble  Dim
dblPerimeter As Double
Dim dblArea As Double

dblLength =[txtRLength]
dblHeight =[txtRHeight]
'              Calculate the perimeter of therectangle
'              by  adding  the  length  to  the  height,  2  timeseach
dblPerimeter  =  2  *  (dblLength  +  dblHeight)  dblArea  =  dblLength
*dblHeight
```

```
[txtRPerimeter] = dblPerimeter
[txtRArea] = dblArea End
Sub

Private Sub cmdECalculate_Click()

Dim  dblRadius1,  dblRadius2  As  Double  Dim
dblCircumference, dblArea AsDouble

dblRadius1 =[txtEllipseRadius1]
dblRadius2 =[txtEllipseRadius2]
dblCircumference = (dblRadius1 + dblRadius2) *3.14159 dblArea = dblRadius1
* dblRadius2 * 3.14159

[txtEllipseCircumference] = dblCircumference
[txtEllipseArea]  =  dblArea  End
Sub
```

2.   In the Object combo box, select **cmdECalculate** and implement itsevent

3.   Return to the form. Test the rectangle and theellipse

The Collection Operator!

The objects used in Microsoft Access are grouped in categories called collections. The forms belong to a collection of objects called **Forms**. The reports belong to a collection of objects called **Reports.** Therefore, all forms of your database project belong to the **Forms** collection.

To call a particular form in an operation, using the exclamation point operator, type Forms followed by the! Operator, followed by the name of the form you need to use. An example would be **Forms!ListOfEmployees** which means the ListOfEmployees form of the **Forms** collection. If the name of the form is made of more than one word, or for convenience (strongly suggested), you must use s square brackets to delimit the name of the form. Therefore, the form would be access with **Forms! [ListOf Employees]**

Practical Learning: Using the Exclamation Operator

1.   GettotheCodeEditorandchangethecodeofthe**cmdSqCalculate_Click**eventasfollows:

Private   SubcmdSqCalculate_Click()   Dim
dblSide AsDouble
Dim dblPerimeter AsDouble Dim
dblArea AsDouble

dblSide = **Forms!frmAlgebraicOperators!txtSqSide**
' Calculate the perimeter of a square by adding the side 4 times dblPerimeter = 4 * dblSide
dblArea = dblSide ^ 2

Forms!frmAlgebraicOperators!txtSqPerimeter = dblPerimeter
Forms!frmAlgebraicOperators!txtSqArea =dblArea End Sub

2.   GetbacktotheformandenteravalueintheSidetextboxofthesquareintheQuadrilateral tab

The Line Continuation Operator: _

You will regularly need to expand your code on more than two lines. This happens regularly if you are writing an expression that involves many entities that must belong to a group.

To continue a piece of code from one line to the next, type an empty space followed by an underscore symbol, then continue your code on the next line

Practical Learning: Using the Underscore Operator

1.   In the Code Editor, click the arrow of the Object combo box and select **cmdCubeCalculate_Click**

2.   Implement the Click event as follows:

Private   Sub   cmdCubeCalculate_Click()
Forms!frmAlgebraicOperators!txtCubeArea = **6***
Forms!frmAlgebraicOperators!txtCubeSide _
*

```
Forms!frmAlgebraicOperators!txtCubeSide
Forms!frmAlgebraicOperators!txtCubeVolume =
Forms!frmAlgebraicOperators!txtCubeSide * _
Forms!frmAlgebraicOperators!txtCubeSide * _ Forms!frmAlgebraicOperators!txtCubeSide
End Sub
```

3.   IntheObjectcombobox,selectcmdBoxCalculateandimplementitsClickeventasfollows:

```
Private Sub cmdBoxCalculate_Click()
' Volume = Length * Width * Height
Forms!frmAlgebraicOperators!txtBoxVolume  =  _  Forms!frmAlgebraicOperators!txtBoxLength  * _
Forms!frmAlgebraicOperators!txtBoxWidth * _ Forms!frmAlgebraicOperators!txtBoxHeight

Dim  dblLength,  dblHeight,  dblWidth  As  Double  dblLength
=Forms!frmAlgebraicOperators!txtBoxLength        dblHeight       =
Forms!frmAlgebraicOperators!txtBoxWidth         dblWidth        =
Forms!frmAlgebraicOperators!txtBoxHeight ' Area = 2 * ((L * H) + (H *
W) + (L *W))
Forms!frmAlgebraicOperators!txtBoxArea = 2 * ( _


End Sub
```

4.   Return to the form and switch it to FormView.

5.   Click the 3-Dimensions tab and test boxshapes:

6.   Save the form and closeit

The Period Operator:

In the next lesson, we will learn about properties of a object. We will find out that a property is something that describes an object. For example, users mainly use a text box either to read the text it contains, or to change its content, by changing the existing text or by entering new text. Therefore, the text the user types in a text box is a property of the text box.

To access the property of an object, type the name of the object, followed by a period, followed by the name of the property you need. The property you are trying to use must be part of the properties of the object. In Microsoft

Access, to use a property of a an object, you must know, either based on experience or with certainty, that the property exists. In Visual Basic, the Code Editor is very helpful and would display the list of properties once you type the period:

Period:

If you know the name of the property, you can start typing it. Once the desired property is highlighted, press the Spacebar or Tab.

If you see the name of the property in the list, you can double-click click it.

If the list doesn't appear, which will happen sometimes for any reason (with experience, you will find out why), press Ctrl + Spacebar.

If you don't want to use the list displayed by the Code Editor, press Esc.

Once you have specified what property you want to use, you can assign it the desired value or you can involve it in any operation you see fit.

Constants

A constant is a value that doesn't change (this definition is redundant because the word value already suggests something that doesn't change). There are two types of constant you will use in your programs: those supplied to you and those you define yourself.

The Carriage Return-Line Feed Constant

Visual Basic provides the vbCrLf constant. It is used to interrupt a line of text and move to the next line.

Built-in Constants: PI

PI is a mathematical constant whose value is approximately equal to 3.1415926535897932. It is highly used in operations that involve circles or geometric variants of a circle: cylinder, sphere, cone, etc.

Built-in Logical Constants: NULL

A variable is said to be null when its value is invalid or doesn't bear any significant or recognizable value.

An expression is said to be false if the result of its comparison is 0. Otherwise, the expression is said to bear a true result.

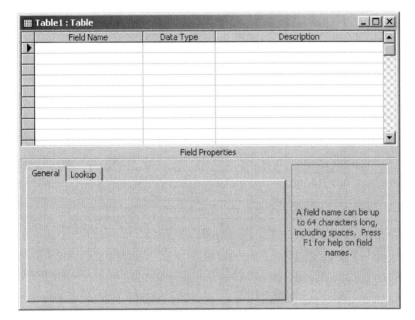

Once in Design View, you must specify a name for each field

Fields Names

Each field on a database must have a name (this is also true for anything in the computer). The name held by a field allows you, the database developer, and the operating system, to refer to that particular field.

To specify the name of a field, type a name in the Field Name column of the table in Design View (The name of a field can also be specified in Datasheet View). There are rules and suggestions used to specify a name for a field. A field name

- Must begin with a letter (a-z or A-Z)
- Cannot contain a period (.) or a special character
- Must not contain a space
- Must not exceed 255 characters. You should limit the name of a variable to 30 characters

• Must be uni☐ue in the same scope

A field can have almost any name such as "first name", "Employee's first name", "First name of the employee", and etc.

On our database, that is, on the fields we create here:

• The name of each field will be made of one word, no space
• The name of a field will start in uppercase; examples are Address, Category, or Format
• If the name of a field is a combination of words, such as First and Name, or Date and of and Birth, instead of writing the whole name indistinctly, each component of the common name will start in uppercase. Instead of Firstname, we will use FirstName. Instead of Dateofbirth, we will use Date Of Birth.

• DateOfBirth.

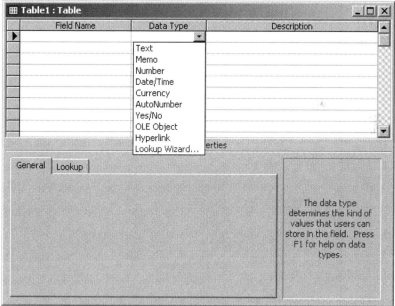

After specifying a name of the field, you can decide what type of data can be entered into that field. The types of data are organized in categories. To specify a data type, click under the Data Type column. This displays an arrow that indicates that this column is in fact made of combo boxes:

Tables Data Types

A **Text** data type allows the user to type any kind of character or group of characters. The field can hold up to 255 characters.

The **Memo** data type functions like the Text except that it can hold up to 64000 characters.

The **Number** data type allows a combination of digits using 0 to 9. As you will see shortly, there are various types of numbers. You will get to specify further number formats you need for your database.

The **Date/Time** data type allows you to control data entry to some fields for a recognizable date or time values. There are various formats used.

The **Currency** data type will accept only a number in its field. That number is then converted to represent monetary value.

Data Type	Used For	Examples
Text	Group of characters of any kind, but it is limited to 255 characters	AC Milan John
Memo	Larger text with a maximum of 64000 Characters	*A text document*
Number	Numeric data	212
Date/Time	Date or time	12/26/90 1:00 PM
Currency	Currency (money) value	$ 34,000
AutoNumber	Setting numeric values automatically	1, 2, 3, 4
OLE Object	Other kinds of files in your database	
Hyperlink	linking from your document to a file in your computer or to a web page on the Internet	www.pbs.org www.atl.com
Lookup Wizard	Predefined data on a particular column. These data are usually prepared by you	

You use the **AutoNumber** data type to ask Microsoft Access to complete that field with automatically generated numbers for a field whose numbers you don't need to control.

An **OLE Object** field allows you to include pictures, graphics, other application files (for example Microsoft Word documents or Microsoft Excel spreadsheets, etc).

With the **Hyperlink**, you can provide a link to a file on your computer or to a web page on the Internet.

The **Lookup Wizard** specifies some predefined data for a particular column. These data are usually prepared by you.

Tabular Description of Data Types

Practical Learning: Designing a Table

1.	Start Microsoft Access and open the **CPAP Help Desk1** database that you created previously.

2.	If the Database Window is not present, press F11. In the Database Window, clickTables.
In the Tables section or Tables property sheet, click the New button

3.	In the New Table dialog box, click Design View and clickOK.

4.	Notice that the first field under Field Name has focus. Type TimeSheetID and pressTab

5.	Click the arrow of the Data Type combo box and selectAutoNumber

6.	Right-click **TimeSheetID** and click PrimaryKey

7.	Click the first field under **Description** and type **Automatic number set by the database**

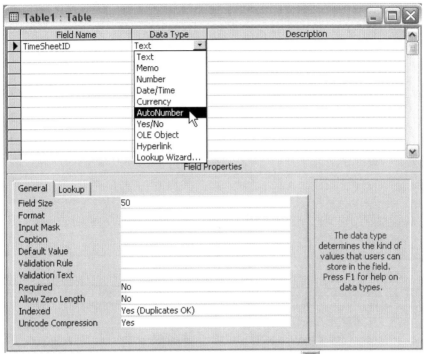

8.   To save the table, on the Table Design toolbar, click the Save button [save icon].

9.   Type **tblTimeSheet** and pressEnter.

10.   Click the first field under **TimeSheetID** and typeEnteredBy

11.   Press the down arrow key. Notice that the Data Type for the **EnteredBy** field is set toText.

12.   Type DateEntered and pressEnter

13.   In the Data Type combo box, select**Date/Time**

14.   Complete the table asfollows:

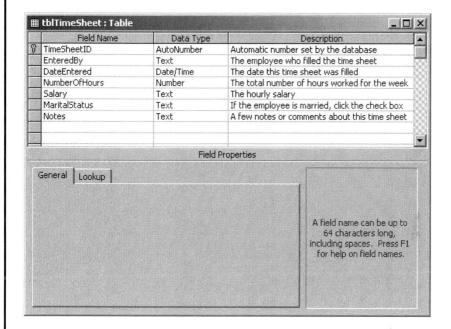

Field Name	Data Type	Description
TimeSheetID	AutoNumber	Automatic number set by the database
EnteredBy	Text	The employee who filled the time sheet
DateEntered	Date/Time	The date this time sheet was filled
NumberOfHours	Number	The total number of hours worked for the week
Salary	Text	The hourly salary
MaritalStatus	Text	If the employee is married, click the check box
Notes	Text	A few notes or comments about this time sheet

Field Properties

General | Lookup

A field name can be up to 64 characters long, including spaces. Press F1 for help on field names.

15. To switch the table to the other view, on the main menu, click View -> DatasheetView.

16. When asked whether you want to save the table, clickYes.

17. After viewing the table, closeit.

Chapter Four
Introduction To Variables

If you create a simple desktop database, the data types and fields in Microsoft Access are sufficient. To customize the behaviors of your fields for a functionality you cannot implement in Microsoft Access, you will use Microsoft Visual Basic as a programming language.

The computer memory is made of small storage areas used to hold the things or components that a program needs while it is running. As a programmer, you specify these things, or you provide them to the computer; the computer then puts them in its storage areas. When you need one of them, you let the computer know. The machine "picks it up", brings it to you, and then you can use it as you see fit.

In the world of computer programming, a variable is a value you ask the computer to temporarily store in its memory while the program is running.

Declaring a Variable

In order to reserve that storage area, you have to let the computer know. Letting the computer know is referred to as Declaring the variable. You declare a variable using the Dim keyword, like this:

Dim

Just like any of the controls we have used so far, a variable needs to have a name. There are rules you should follow when naming your variables. The name of a variable:

• Must begin with an letter
• After starting with an letter, can be made of letters, underscores, and digits in another order
• Cannot have a period
• Can have up to 255 characters.
• Must be uni ue inside of the event (or procedure, function or module (we will learn what these things are)) it is used in.

To name, a variable, follow the same rules and suggestions we used for a table's fields.

To declare a variable, locate the event that you want to use the variable in. Follow the above syntax and the below suggestions and data types.

Visual Basic Data Types

Just like you specify a data type for a table's field, you also specify a data type for a variable. This time, a data type tells the computer what kind of variable you are going to use in your program. There are different kinds of variables for various purposes. Before assigning a data type to a variable, you should know how much space a data type will occupy in memory. Different variables or different data types use different amount of space in memory. The amount of space used by a data type is measured in bytes.

Most of the data types you use in Visual Basic correspond to those you used in Microsoft Access and are easily recognizable.

String

A **String** in Visual Basic is used for characters such as names and text of any kind and almost any length. It can be used for a Microsoft Access **Text** or **Memo** data types. To declare a string data type, for example when a form opens, here is an example:

Private Sub Form_Load()
Dim CountryName As String
End Sub

Boolean

In Microsoft Access, you can specify a field as providing a Yes or No, a True or False, an On or Off, a 1 or 0 values. Its Microsoft Access corresponding type is the **Boolean** data type. Here is an example of declaring a Boolean variable when the form opens:

Private Sub Form_Load()
Dim CountryName As String
Dim IsMarried As Boolean
End Sub

Byte

If you are planning to use a number in your program, you have a choice from different kinds of numbers that Visual Basic can recognize. You can use the same **Byte** data type which is a natural number that ranges from 0 to 255. You can declare it as follows:

Private Sub Form_Load()

```
Dim CountryName As String Dim
IsMarried    As    Boolean    Dim
StudentAge As Byte

EndSub
```

Integer

An Integer is a number that ranges from -32,768 to 32,767. It is the same Integer used in Microsoft Access. It is the same integer used in Microsoft Access. The integer type should always be used when counting things such as books in a library or students in a school; in this case, you would not use decimal values. Here is an example of declaring an integer variable:

```
Private Sub Form_Load()
Dim  CountryName  As  String
Dim IsMarried As Boolean Dim
StudentAge   As   Byte    Dim
Tracks AsInteger
End Sub
```

Long

A Long integer is a number that can be used for a field or variable involving greater numbers than integers. The Long type is also suitable for numbers that don't involve decimal values. You can use the Long type as corresponding to the AutoNumber used in Microsoft Access (as long as you are not using it as Replication ID), although the AutoNumber was a Long Integer. Here is an example where a Long integer variable isdeclared:

```
Private Sub Form_Load()
Dim  CountryName  As  String
Dim IsMarried As Boolean Dim
StudentAge   As   Byte   Dim
Tracks    As     IntegerDim
Population AsLong
End Sub
```

Single

A **Single** is a decimal floating number. Unlike an integer or a **Long** integer, a **Single** variable can have a decimal portion such as 12.44 or 804.60. Here is an example of declaring a **Single** floating variable:

```
Private Sub Form_Load()
Dim  CountryName  As  String
Dim IsMarried As Boolean Dim
StudentAge  As  Byte  Dim
Tracks AsInteger


Dim Population AsLong
```
Dim Distance AsSingle
```
EndSub
```

Double

A **Double** data type should be used for a variable that carries (or would carry) a decimal value. This data type is similar to Microsoft Access' Double.

In most circumstances, it is preferable to use **Double** instead of **Single** when declaring a variable that would hold a decimal number. Although the **Double** takes more memory spaces (computer memory is not expensive any more (!)), it provides more precision.

Here is an example of declaring a Double variable:

```
Private Sub Form_Load()
```
Dim Distance As Double
```
End Sub
```

Currency

The **Currency** data type is used to deal with currency values the same way the Currency is used in MS Access. Here is an example of declaring it:

```
Private Sub Form_Load ()
```

```
Dim CountryName As String
Dim IsMarried As Boolean Dim
StudentAge    As    Byte    Dim
Tracks    As    Integer    Dim
Population    As    Long    Dim
Distance AsSingle
```
Dim StartingSalary As Currency
```
End Sub
```

Date

In Microsoft Access, a Date/Time data type is used to control a field with a date or a time values. In Visual Basic, a **Date** data type is used to specify a date or time value. Therefore, in Microsoft Visual Basic, to declare either a date or a time variables, use the **Date** keyword. Here are two examples:

```
Private Sub Form_Load ()
Dim CountryName As String Dim
IsMarried As Boolean

Dim StudentAge As Byte
Dim Tracks As Integer
Dim Population As Long
Dim Distance As Single
Dim StartingSalary As Currency
```
Dim DateOfBirth As Date
Dim KickOffTime As Date
```
EndSub
```

Object

An **Object** is almost anything else that you want to use in your program. If you don't specify a data type or can't figure out what data type you want to use, you can use the Variant or let Visual Basic use the Variant data type.

Variant

A **Variant** can be used to declare any kind of variable. You can use a variant when you can't make up your mind regarding a variable but, as a beginning programmer, you should avoid it.

Here is a table of various data types and the amount of memory space each one uses:

Datatype	Description	Range
Byte	1-byte binary data	0 to 255
Integer	2-byte integer	$-32,768$ to $32,767$
Long	4-byte integer	$-2,147,483,648$ to $2,147,483,647$
Single	4-byte floating-point number	$-3.402823E38$ to $-1.401298E-45$ (negative values)
		$1.401298E-45$ to $3.402823E38$ (positive values)
Double	8-byte floating-point number	$-1.79769313486231E308$ to $-4.94065645841247E-324$ (negative values)
		$4.94065645841247E-324$ to $1.79769313486231E308$ (positive values)
Currency	8-byte number with fixed decimal point	$-922,337,203,685,477.5808$ to $922,337,203,685,477.5807$
String	String of characters	Zero to approximately two billion characters
Variant	Date/time, floating-point number, integer, string, or object. 16 bytes, plus 1 byte for each character if a string value.	Date values: January 1, 100 to December 31, 9999 Numeric values: same range as **Double** String values: same range as **String** Can also contain **Error** or **Null** values
Boolean	2 bytes	**True** or **False**
Date	8-byte date/time value	January 1, 100 to December 31, 9999

Object	4 bytes	Any **Object** reference

We have learned how to declare a variable as follows:

Dim CountryName **As**String

We also saw that we can declare different variables each on its own line asfollows;

Dim FirstName
AsString **Dim**
LastName **As**String
Dim Salary **As**
Currency
Dim AlreadyVisited **As**Boolean

If you have many variables of the same data type, you can declare them on the same line, each separated with a comma; remember to specify their common type. Here is an example:

Private Sub Form_Load()
Dim CountryName, Address, City, State As String
Dim IsMarried As
Boolean Dim
StudentAge As Byte
Dim Tracks As
Integer Dim
Population As Long
Dim Distance As
Single
Dim StartingSalary, WeeklyEarnings As Currency Dim
DateOfBirth, KickOffTime As Date
End Sub

When naming your variables, besides the above suggestions, you can start a variable's name with a one to three letter prefix that could identify the data type used. Here are a few suggestions

Data Type	Prefix	Example
Boolean	bln	blnFound
Byte	byt	bytTracks
Date/Time	dtm	dteStartOfShift
Double	dbl	dblDistance
Error	err	errCantOpen
Integer	int	intNbrOfStudents
Long	lng	lngPopulation
Object	obj	objConnection
Single	sng	sngAge
String	str	strCountryName
Currency	cur	curHourlySalary
Variant	var	varFullName

CHAPTER FIVE
Modules, Procedures, and Functions

Modules

A module is file that holds code or pieces of code that belong either to a form, a report, or is simply considered as an independent unit of code. This independence means that a unit may also not belong to a particular form o rreport. Each form or repor thasa (separate) module. To access the module of a form or report, open the object in Design View and click the Code button . If you initiate the coding of an event of a form (or report) or of a control that is positioned on the form, this would open the Code Editor window and display the module that belongs to the form (orreport).If no code has been written for the form or report, its module would beempty:

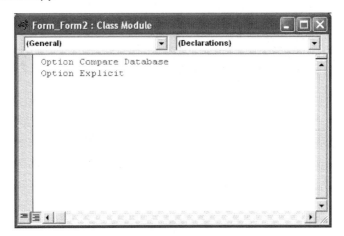

If you have writte nevents for a form (orreport) or for the controls that belong to the form (or report), all these events would b epart of the form's (orreport's) module.

Besides the modules that belong to forms (orreports), you can create your own module that are not related to a particular form (orreport). There are three main ways you can create an independent module:

- In Microsoft Access, on the Data base Window, click Modules and clickNew. This would open the Code Editor with an emptyfile.

- In the Code Editor (or Microsoft Visual Basic) window, on the main menu, click Insert-> Module

- In the Code Editor (or Microsoft Visual Basic) tool bar, you can click the Insert Module button or click the arrow of the Insert Module but to nand select Module.

The name of modules are cumulative. This means that the first module would be called Module1; the second would be Module2, etc. It is a good idea to have names that are explic it especially if your application ends up with various modules. Touse acustomname for a module, you musts aveit.This would prompty out on a me the module.You can accept the suggested name or type your own and press Enter.

1. Start Microsoft Access and open the **Bethesda Car Rental3**database

2. On the Database Window, click Modules and clickNew

3. Tosavethemodule,onthetoolbar,clicktheSavebutton

4. Type**modAssignments**andpressEnter.Noticethenameofthemoduleonthetitlebar.

5. Openthe**VBAccess1**application.OntheDatabaseWindow,ifnecessary,clickForms

6. Double-clickthe**frmProcedures**formtoopenitinFormView.Afterviewingtheform, switch it to DesignView

7. The accomp any in gresources include pictures of geometric figures. To enhance the form, you can them. To do that, on the Toolbox, click Image and click the left area of the labels. On the Insert Picture dialog box, locate the picture and addit.

8. To start a form module, with the form open edin Design View, on the Form Design tool bar, click the Code button

Sub Procedures

A procedure is an assignment you ask Microsoft Visual Basic to perform besides, or to complete, then or malflow of the program. A procedure is created to work in conjunction with the control sevent so fadata base. Structurally, aprocedure appears similar to an event.The main difference is that, while an event belongs to a control, a procedure doesn't. While an event is specific to the user's intervention or interaction with a control, a procedure can be general and applied anyway youlike.

Creating a Procedure Manually

There are two kinds of procedures in Microsoft Visual Basic: A subprocedure and a function. The difference lies on their behaviors buttheirco ding (programming) depends of your goal.

A subprocedure is a section of code that carries an assignment butdoesn't give back aresult. To create a subprocedure, start the section of code with the **Sub** keyword followed by a name for the sub procedure. To differentiate the name of the sub procedure with any other regular name, it must be followed by an opening and closing parent heses. The **Sub** keyword and the name of the procedure (including its parentheses) are written on one line (by default). The section of the sub procedure code closes with **End Sub** asfollows:

```
Sub
Sho
wM
e()
End
Sub
```

The name of a subprocedure should follow the same rules we learned to name the variables, omitting theprefix:

- If the subprocedure perform sanaction that can be represented with a verb, you can use that verb to name it. Here are examples: show,display

- To make the name of a subprocedure stand, you should start it in uppercase. Examples are Show, Play, Dispose,Close

- You should use explicit names that identify the purpose of the sub procedure. If a procedure would be used as a resul to fan other procedure or a control' sevent, reflectiton the name of the subprocedure. Examples would be: after update, long before.

- If the name of aprocedure is a combination fwords, start each word in uppercase. Examples are: After Update, Say It Loud

The section between the first Sub line and the End Sub line is called the body of the sub routine. In the body of aprocedure, you define what the procedure is supposed to do. If you need to use a variable, you can declare it and specify what kind of variable you need. There is no restriction on the type of variables that can be declared in aprocedure. Here is an example in which as tring variable is declare din the body of a subprocedure:


```
Sub Create Name ()
Dim strFullName As String
End Sub
```

In the same way, you can declare as many variable as you need inside of a sub procedure. Theactionsyouperforminsideofaproceduredependonwhatyouaretryingtoaccomplish. Forexample, a subprocedure can be simply be used to create as tring. The above procedure can be changed asfollows:

```
Sub CreateName()
Dim strFullName As String
strFullName = "Jacques Fame Ndongo"
End Sub
```

Similarly, aprocedure can be used to perform a simple calculation such as adding two numbers. Here is anexample:

```
Sub Calculate Total Students ()
Dim StudentsInClass1 AsInteger Dim
StudentsInClass2 AsInteger
Dim TotalNumberOfStudents As Integer

StudentsInClass1 =32
StudentsInClass2 =36
TotalNumberOfStudents = StudentsInClass1 +StudentsInClass2
End Sub
```

There are two main ways a subprocedure receives values. To start, aprocedure that is written in the module of a form (or report) has direct access to the controls that belong to the form (orreport). This means that the procedure can call them and manipulate any of their available properties. Here is an example of a procedure implemented in a form that has a text box calledtxtCountry:

```
Sub ChangeColor()
txtCountry.BackColor = 16763293
```

End Sub

In the same way, you can declare variables and perform operations inside of aprocedure and hand the result to a control that is part of a form orreport.

1.   Click the first empty line in the Code Editor and type **Sub Square Solution** and press Enter

2.   Notice that Visual Basic added the End Sub line and positioned the cursorinside the procedure.

3.   Complete the sub procedure asfollows:

Sub Square Solution ()
'   Declare the necessary variables for thesquare
Dim dblSide As Double
Dim dblPerimeter, dblArea As Double

'   Retrieve the value of theside
dblSide = txtSqSide
'   Calculate the perimeter and the are of thesquare
dblPerimeter = dblSide * 4 dblArea =
dblSide *dblSide
'   Preparetodisplaytheresultintheappropriatetextboxes
txtSqPerimeter =dblPerimeter txtSqArea
= dblArea
End Sub

4.   Return to Microsoft Access and switch the form to Form View. Enter a value in the Side text box of the square and click the Calculate button. Notice that nothing happens.

Inserting Procedure

Microsoft Visual Basic simplifies the creation of aprocedure through the use of the Insert Procedure dialogbox:

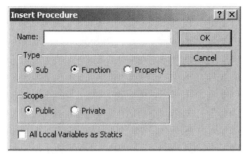

To display the Insert Procedure, you can click Insert->Procedure on the main menu, or click the arrow of the Insert Procedure button on the tool bar. If you are creating a subprocedure,

Click the Sub radio button. If you want the procedure to be access only by the objects, events and procedure of the same module, click the Private radio button. If you want to access the procedure from outside of the current module, click the Public radio button.

Practical Learning: Inserting a Procedure

1. Switch the form back to Design View and access the Code Editor. On the main menu, click Insert ->Procedure...

2. On the Insert Procedure dialog box, click the Name text box and type **Solve Rectangle**

3. In the Type section, click the Sub radiobutton.

4. In the Scope section, click the Private radiobutton

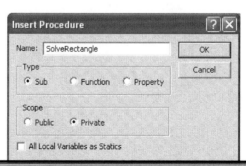

5. ClickOK

6. Implement the procedure asfollows:

Private Sub SolveRectangle()
'   Declare the necessary variables for therectangle
Dim   dblLength,   dblHeight   As   Double
DimdblPerimeter,dblAreaAsDouble

'   Retrieve the values of the length andheight
dblLength   =txtRLength
dblHeight =txtRHeight
'   Calculate the perimeter and the area of therectangle
dblPerimeter=(dblLength+dblHeight)*2 dblArea = dblLength
*dblHeight
'   Prepare to display the result in the appropriate text boxes
txtRPerimeter =dblPerimeter txtRArea =
dblArea
End Sub

Calling a Procedure

After creating a procedure, you can call it from another procedure, function, orcontrol's event. To call as impleprocedure such as the above Change Color, you can just write the name of the subprocedure. Here is an example where a subprocedure is called when a form is clicked.

Private Sub Detail_Click()
ChangeColor
End Sub

Practical Learning: Calling a Procedure

1. In the Object combo box, selectcmdSqCalculate

2. Call the SolveSquare procedure asfollows:

Private Sub cmdSqCalculate_Click()

SquareSolution

End Sub

3.   In the Object combo box, select cmdR Calculate and implement its Click event follows:

Private Sub cmdRCalculate_Click()

SolveRectangle

End Sub

4.   Return to Microsoft Access and switch the form to FormView.

5.   In the Side text box of the square, type14.55 and click the right Calculate button

6.   Also text the rectangle with18.25 for the lengt hand15.75 for the height and click its Calculate button:

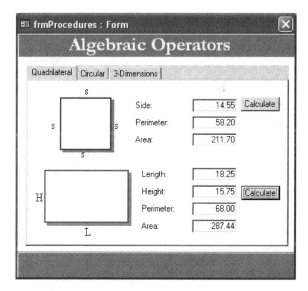

7.   Save the form and return to the CodeEditor

Function Procedures

A function is aprocedure that takes care of are latively small assignment on aside and returns aresult. A function esembles asubprocedure in all respects except that a function returnsa value.

Creating a Function

A function is created like asubprocedure with a few more rules. The creation of a function starts with the keyword **Function** and closes with **End Function**. Here is an example:

FunctionGetFu
llName()   End
Function

The name of the function follows the same rule sand suggestions we have reviewed for the sub procedures. Because a function should return a value, after the parentheses, type the **As** keyword followed by the type of data the function must return. Here is an example:

FunctionGetFullName()AsString
EndFunction

The implementation of a function is done the same way that of a subprocedure is. Becausea function is supposed to return a value, after performing what ever assignment you need in a function, you can assign the desired result to the name of the function before the closing of the function. Here is

anexample:

Function GetFullName() As String
DimstrFirstName,strLastNameAsString
strFirstName = txtFirstName strLastName
=txtLastName
GetFullName = strFirstName & " " &strLastName

End Function

Practical Learning: Creating a Function

1.   In the Code Editor, scroll down, click the first empty line, type **Function Circle Circumference As Double** and press Enter

2.   Notice that Visual Basic completed the code with the **End Function** line and positioned the cursorin the body of the function. Implement the function as follows:

Function CircleCircumference() As Double

Dim dblRadius As Double

dblRadius   =   txtCircleRadius
CircleCircumference=dblRadius*2*3.14159
End Function

3.   On the main menu, click Insert ->Procedure...

4.   Type **CircleArea** in the Name textbox

5.   In the Type section, make sure the **Function** radio is selected (thedefault). In the Scope section, click the **Private** radio button and clickOK.

6.   Implement the function asfollows:

Private Function Circle Area ()**AsDouble Dim**
dblRadius AsDouble
dblRadius = txtCircleRadius
CircleArea = dblRadius * dblRadius * 3.14159
End Function

Calling a Function

To call a function, you have two main alternatives. If the function was implemented as simple as asubprocedure, you can just write its name in the event or the function that is calling it. If you want to use the return value of a function in an event or another function, assign the name of the function to the appropriate local variable. Here is an example:

Private Sub Detail_DblClick(Cancel As Integer)

txtFullName = GetFullName

End Sub

Practical Learning: Calling a Function

1.   IntheObjectcombobox,selectcmdCCalculateandimplementitsClickeventasfollows:

Private   Sub   cmdCCalculate_Click()
txtCircleCircumference=CircleCircumference   txtCircleArea   =
CircleArea
End Sub

2.   Switch to Microsoft Access and switch the form to FormView.

3.   ClicktheCirculartaband,inthetopRadiustextbox,type**25.55**

4.   Click the right calculate button (for theCircle).

CHAPTER SIX
Accessories for Programming

Introduction

When using a database, you are in fact using two applications to create a final product. Microsoft Access is used to design the necessary objects for your product. This means that Microsoft Access is used for its visual display of objects. On the other hand, Microsoft Visual Basic is used to handle code that enhance the functionality of your application.

The Compiler

The code you write is made of small instructions written in Visual Basic. These instructions are written in English, a language that the computer, that is the operating system, doesn't understand. Visual Basic, as its own language among other computer languages, is internally equipped with a low level program called a compiler. This program takes your English language instructions and translates them in a language the computer can understand. The language the computer speaks is known as the machine language. You usually don't need to know anything about this language.

After writing your code, at one time it is transmitted to the compiler. The compileranalyzesit first, checks its syntax, the words used in the program, the variables are checked for their declaration and use. The events and procedures are checked for their behavior. The expressions are checked for their accuracy. If something is wrong with the code, that is, if the compiler does not understand something in your code, it would display an error and stop. You must correct them is take or else... As long as the compiler cannot figure out a piece of code in a module, it would not valid ate it. If the code is" admissible", the compiler would perform the assignments that are part of the code and give you are sultbased on its interpretation of the code. This means that the code can be accurate but produce anunreliableorfalseresult.This is because the compiler is just another program: it does not think and does not correct mistakes although it can sometimes point them out. For this reason, you should know what you aredoing.

Writing Argumentative Procedures

To carry out an assignment, sometimes aprocedure needs one or more values to work on. Ifa procedure needs avalue, such avalue is called an argument. While acertain procedure might need one argument, another procedure might need many arguments. The number and types of arguments of a procedure depend on yourgoal.

goal.

Anargument is also called aparameter. Both words mean the samething.

If you are writing your own procedure, then you will decide how many arguments your procedure would need. You also decide on the type of the argument (s). For aprocedure that is taking one argument, inside of the parentheses of the procedure, write the name of the argument followed by the **As** key word followed by the type of data of the argument. Here is an example:

SubCalculate Area (**Radius As Double**) EndSub

A procedure can take more than one argument. If you are creating such aprocedure, between the parentheses of the procedure, write the name of the first argument followed by **As**followed by the data type, followed by a comma. Add the second argument and subsequent arguments and close the parentheses. There is no implied relationship between the arguments; for example, they can be of the sametype:

SubCalculate Perimeter (**Length As Double, Height As Double**) EndSub

The arguments of your procedure can also be as varied as you need them to be. Here is an example:

SubDisplay Greetings (**strFullNameAsString, int Age As Integer,dblDistance As Double**)

EndSub

Practical Learning: Writing Procedures With Arguments

1.   Switch to the Code Editor. Click an empty are a at the end of the existing code and create the following procedure:

```
Sub Solve Ellipse (Small Radius As Double, Large Radius As Double) Dim
dblCircum As Double
Dim dblArea As Double

dblCircum    =    (SmallRadius    +    LargeRadius)    *    2
dblArea=SmallRadius*LargeRadius*3.14159

txtEllipseCircumference =dblCircum  txtEllipseArea =
dblArea
End Sub
```

2.   To create an example of function that takes an argument, add the following function at the end of the existing code:

Function Cube Area(Side As Double) AsDouble
CubeArea = Side * Side *6
End Function

3.   To use different examples of functions that take one or two arguments, type the following functions:

```
Function Cube Volume (Side AsDouble) As Double Cube Volume =
Side * Side *Side
End Function

Function BoxArea(dblLength As Double, _
dblHeight As Double, _ dblWidth As Double) AsDouble
Dim Area As Double

Area = 2 * ((dblLength * dblHeight) +_
(dblHeight * dblWidth) +_ (dblLength * dblWidth)_
)
BoxArea  =  Area
End Function
```

```
Function BoxVolume(dblLength As Double, _
dblHeight As Double, _ dblWidth As Double) AsDouble
Dim Volume As Double
Volume=dblLength*dblHeight*dblHeight BoxVolume =Volume
End Function
```

Calling Argumentative Procedures

We saw already how to call aprocedure that does not take any argument. Actually, there are various ways you can call a sub procedure. As we saw already, if a sub procedure does not take an argument, to call it, you can just write its name. If a sub procedure is taking an argument, to call it, type the name of the sub procedure followed by the name of the argument. If the subprocedure is taking more than one argument, tocallit, type the name of the procedure followed by the name of the arguments, in the exact order they are passed to the sub procedure, separated by a comma. Here is anexample:

```
Private SubtxtResult_GotFocus()
Dim dblHours As Double
Dim dblSalary As Double

dblHours       =
txtHours  dblSalary
=txtSalary

CalcAndShowSalary dblHours, dblSalary
End Sub
Sub CalcAndShowSalary(Hours As Double, Salary AsDouble)
Dim dblResult As Double

dblResult = Hours * Salary
txtResult = dblResult
End Sub
```

Alternatively, you canuse the keyword **Call** to call a subprocedure. In this case, when calling a procedure using **Call**, you must include the argument(s) between the parentheses. Using **Call**, the above **Got Focus** event could call the **Calc And Show Salary** as follows:

```
Private SubtxtResult_GotFocus()
Dim dblHours As Double
```

Dim dblSalary As Double

dblHours   =
txtHours   dblSalary
=txtSalary

Call Calc And Show Salary(dblHours, dblSalary)
End Sub

Practical Learning: Calling Procedures With Arguments

1.   To call the above procedures that take arguments, on the Object combo box, select
cmdE Calculate and implement its **On Click** event as follows:

Private Sub cmdECalculate_Click()
Dim   Radius1   AsDouble
Dim Radius2 AsDouble
Radius1 = txtEllipseRadius1 Radius2 =
txtEllipseRadius2   SolveEllipse
Radius1,Radius2
End Sub

2.   On the Object combo box, select **cmd Cube Calculate** and implementits Click event as
follows:

Private Sub cmdCubeCalculate_Click()
Dim dblSide As Double Dim
dblArea As Double Dim
dblVolume AsDouble

dblSide = txtCubeSide dblArea
=CubeArea(dblSide)
dblVolume = CubeVolume(dblSide)

txtCubeArea   =   dblArea
txtCubeVolume =dblVolume

End Sub

3.   On the Object combo box, select **cmdBox Calculate** and implementits Click event as follows:

```
Private Sub cmdBoxCalculate_Click()
Dim dLen AsDouble
Dim dHgt AsDouble
Dim dWdt AsDouble
Dim Area, Vol As Double

dLen  =txtBoxLength
dHgt   =txtBoxHeight
dWdt = txtBoxWidth

Area  =  BoxArea(dLen,  dHgt,  dWdt)
Vol=BoxVolume(dLen,dHgt,dWdt)

txtBoxArea  =  Area
txtBoxVolume =Vol
End Sub
```

4.   Close the Code Editor or Microsoft Visual Basic and return to Microsoft Access.

5.   Switch the form to Form View and test the ellipse in the Circulartab.

6.   Also test the cube and the box in the 3-Dimensionstab

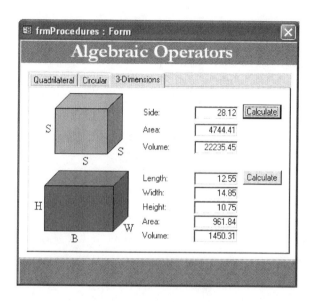

7. Save and close the form

8. Close Microsoft Access

Built-In Functions and Procedures

Introduction

Microsoft Access and Visual Basic ship with an lot of functions and procedures you can use in your database. Before creating your own procedures, you should know what is already available so you don't have to re-invent and waste a great deal of your time. The functions already created are very efficient and were tested in various scenarios so you can use them with complete reliability. The available functions range in various types. There are so many of them that we can only review those that you are most likely to use very often. You can find out about the other in the Help files because they are fairly documented.

Conversion Functions

Anything the user types in a text-based field is primarily considered as a string. Although Microsoft Access and Visual Basic perform a great deal of work behind the scenes to validate the various values that the user provides during data entry, sometimes you will need to make sure that a value is of the type you are expected. This is also valid even if the user did not enter a certain value, you would still need to retrieve a value and convert it to the right data type.

There are various conversion functions adapted to the data types they are dealing with. The general syntax of the conversion functions is:

ReturnType = Function (Expression)

The expression could be of any kind, depending on how the expression would be supplied. For example, it could be a string or value the user would have entered in form. It could also be the result of a calculation performed from other fields on the database. The function would take   such a value, string, or expression and attempt to convert. If the conversion is successful, the function would return an new value that is of the type specified by the *ReturnType in our syntax.*

The conversion functions are as follows:

Function Name	Return Type	Description
CBool	Boolean	Converts an expression into a Boolean value
CByte	Byte	Converts an expression into Byte number
CDate	Date	Converts and expression into a date or time value
CDbl	Double	Converts an expression into a flowing-point (decimal) number
CInt	Integer	Converts an expression into an integer (natural) number
CCur	Currency	Converts an expression into a currency (monetary) value
CLng	Long	Converts an expression into a long integer (a large natural) number
CSng	Single	Converts an expression into a flowing-point (decimal) number
CStr	String	Converts an expression into a string

Creating a Message Box

A message box is a special dialog box used to display a piece of information to the user. As opposed to a regular form, the user cannot type anything on the dialog box. There are usually two kinds of message boxes you will create: one that simply display information and one that expects the user to make a decision.

There are two methods you can use to create a message box using the **MsgBox** function. To display a simple message with just an OK button, use the **MsgBox** method whose formula is

MsgBox [*Message*]

On the other hand, you can ask the message box to display a more informative prompt with more than one button. Then you can write an expression that would perform an action based on the particular button the user clicked. In this case, you would have to use the MsgBox function (not the method).

The syntax of the **MsgBox** function is

MsgBox [*Message*] [*Buttons*] [*Title*] [*HelpFile*] [*Context*]

The **MsgBox** method takes only one argument. The **MsgBox** function takes five arguments. The *Message* argument is required on both.

The *Message* argument is the string that the user will see displaying on the message box. As a string, you can display it in double quotes, like this "That's All Folks". You can also create it from other pieces of strings. The Message argument can be made of up to 1024 characters. To display the *Message* on multiple lines, you can use either the constant **vbCrLf** or the combination **Chr (10) & Chr(13)** between any twostrings.

The *Buttons* argument specifies what button or buttons should display on the message box. There are different kinds of buttons available and Visual Basic recognizes them by a numeric value assigned to each.

The *Buttons* argument can have one of the following constant

Button	Value	Display

Constant	Value	Buttons
vbOKOnly	0	OK
vbOKCancel	1	OK Cancel
vbAbortRetryIgnore	2	Abort Retry Ignore
vbYesNoCancel	3	Yes No Cancel
vbYesNo	4	Yes No
vbRetryCancel	5	Retry Cancel

From the buttons on the message box, you can decide which one would be the default, that is, which button would be activated if the user presses Enter instead of clicking. You can set the default argument using the following table

Option	Value
vbDefaultButton1	0
vbDefaultButton2	256
vbDefaultButton3	512
vbDefaultButton4	768

These additional buttons can be used to further control what the user cando:

Constant	Value
vbApplicationModal	0
vbSystemModal	4096

In addition to the buttons, you can use the following icons on the messagebox

Icon	Value	Description
vbCritical	16	
vbQuestion	32	
vbExclamation	48	

vbInformation	64	

The *Title* argument is the caption that would display in the title bar of the message box. It is a string whose word or words you can enclose between parentheses or that you can get from a created string.

If your application is using a help file, you can specify this and let the message box use it. The *HelpFile* argument is a string that specifies the name of the help file, and the Context argument provides the number that corresponds to the appropriate help topic for the message box.

As a function, the **MsgBox** function is useful for the value it returns. This value corresponds to the button the user clicks on the message box. Depending on the buttons the message box is displaying after the user has clicked, the **MsgBox** function can return one of the following values:

Button	Return	Value
OK	**vbOK**	1
Cancel	**vbCancel**	2
	vbAbort	3
Retry	**vbRetry**	4
Ignore	**vbIgnore**	5
	vbYes	6
No	**vbNo**	7

Practical Learning: Creating Message Boxes

1. Open the VBAccess1 application and, on the Database Window, clickForms

2. Double-click the Messages form to openit

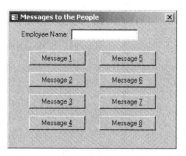

3. Switch the form to DesignView.

4. Right-click the Message 1 button and click Build Event... On the Choose Builder dialog box, click Code Builder and clickOK

5. In the Code Editor, implement it asfollows:

Private Sub cmdMessage1_Click ()
MsgBox "This is Visual Basic as simple as it canget"
End Sub

6. To test the form, return to Microsoft Access and switch the form to FormView.

7. On the form, click the Message 1button.

8. Notice that a message box displays. Also notice the caption on the title bar displays MicrosoftAccess.

9. Click OK to close the messagebox.

10. Switch the form back to Design View and return to the CodeEditor

11. Instead of the title bar displaying Microsoft Access as the caption, you can set your own caption. This is done through the 3rd argument of the **MsgBox** function. To see an example, on the Object combo box, select cmdMessage2 and implement its Click event as follows:

Private Sub cmdMessage2_Click ()
MsgBox "Before formatting a floppy disk, "& _ "make sure you
know its content", , _ "Disk Formatting Instructions"
End Sub

12. Test the form and the Message 2 button. Then return to the CodeEditor

13. When creating a message box using the **MsgBox** function, you can decide which button you want to use, using one of the constants we have listedearlier.
To see an example, on the Object combo box, select cmdMessage3 and implement its Click event as follows:

```
Private Sub cmdMessage3_Click ()
MsgBox "This will be your only warning", _ vbOKOnly +
vbExclamation, _ "Attention! Attention!!Attention!!!"
End Sub
```

14.   Test the form and the Message 3 button. Return to the CodeEditor

15.   If you want to display a message on different lines, you can use the **vbCrLf** constant. As an example, on the Object combo box, select cmdMessage4 and implement its Click event as follows:

```
Private Sub cmdMessage4_Click ()
MsgBox "You are about to embark on a long journey." & _ vbCrLf & "If
your courage is still fresh, "& _ "now is the time to let us know!", _
vbOKCancel + vbQuestion, _ "Accept or Cancel
theMission"
End Sub
```

16.   TesttheformandexperimentwiththeMessage4button.ThenreturntotheCodeEditor.

17.   You can also display a message on various lines using the **Chr ()** function. To see an example, on the Object combo box, select cmdMessage5 and implement its Click event as follows:

```
Private Sub cmdMessage5_Click ()
MsgBox "This message usually appears when trying "&_
"to format a floppy disk while the floppy drive " & _ "is empty. " &Chr(13) & Chr(10)
& _
"When or if this happens, make sure you have a " & _ " floppy disk in the floppy
drive.", _ vbAbortRetryIgnore + vbCritical,_
"Floppy Disk Formatting"
End Sub
```

18.   Test the form and the Message 5 button. Then return to the CodeEditor.

19.   The usefulness of the **MsgBox** function is demonstrated in your ability to perform an action based on

the button the user has clicked on the message box. Indeed, the implementations we have used so far were on the MsgBox method. If you want to get the button that the user has clicked, you have to use the function itself. The true capture of the clicked button is revealed by your finding out the clicked button. This is done using conditional statements that we have not learned so far. Therefore, we will just learn how to implement the function and how to assign a response button to it; throughout this tutorial, and when ever necessary, we will eventually see what to do when a certain button has been clicked. To see an example, on the Object combo box, select cmdMessage6 and implement its Click event as follows:

Private Sub cmdMessage6_Click ()
Dim intResponse As Integer

intResponse = MsgBox("Your printing configuration " & _
"is not fully set." & vbCrLf & _
"If you are ready to print, click" & vbCrLf & _   "(1) Yes: To print the document anyway" & vbCrLf &
_ "(2) No: To configure printing" & vbCrLf &_
"(3) Cancel: To dismiss printing", _ vbYesNoCancel + vbInformation, _ "Critical
Information")
End Sub

20.   Test the form and the Message 6 button. Then return to the CodeEditor

21.   When a message box displays, one of the buttons, if more than one is displaying, has a thicker border than the other(s); such a button is called the default button. By default, this is the 1st or most left button on the message box. If you want to control which button would be the default, use one of the default constant buttons listed above. To see an example, on the Object combo box, select cmdMessage7 and implement its Click event as follows:

Private Sub cmdMessage7_Click()
Dim intAnswer As Integer

intAnswer = MsgBox("Do you want to continue this " & _ "operation?", _
vbYesNoCancel + vbQuestion + vbDefaultButton2, _ "National Inquiry")
End Sub

22. Test the form and the Message 7 button. Then return to the CodeEditor.

23. Although the user cannot type on a message box, not only can you decide what it displays, but you can also use string variables that would be available only when the form is running. As an example, on the Object combo box, select cmdMessage8 and implement its Click event asfollows:

```
Private Sub cmdMessage8_Click()
Dim strEmplName As String Dim
intInquiry As Integer

strEmplName = CStr(txtEmployeeName)
intInquiry = MsgBox("Hi, " & strEmplName & Chr(13) &_
"I think we met already." & vbCrLf & _
"I don't know when. I don't know where." & vbCrLf & _ "I don't know why. But I bet we met
somewhere.", _ vbYesNo + vbInformation, _
"Meeting Acquaintances")

End Sub
```

24. To test the form, return to Microsoft Access

25. On the Employee Name text box, type JanetDouglas

26. Click the Message 8 button and see the result.

27. Click one of the buttons to close the message box.

28. Close the running form, click its close button.

Data Request With the Input Box

Although most of the user's data entry will be performed on fields positioned on a form, Microsoft Visual Basic provides a function that allows you to request a piece of information to the user who can type it in a text field of a dialog box. The function used to accomplish this is called InputBox and its basic syntax is:

InputBox (*prompt*)

The most basic piece of information you should provide to the InputBox function is referred to as the prompt. It should be a string that the user will read and know what you are expecting. Here is an example:

Private Sub cmdRequestDOB_ Click ()
InputBox "Enter your date of birth as mm/dd/yyyy" End Sub

This would produce

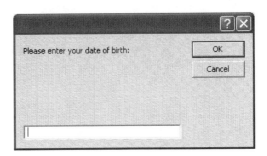

Upon reading the message on the Input box, the user is asked to enter a piece of information. The type of information the user is supposed to provide depends on you, the programmer.

Therefore, there are two important things you should always do. First, you should let the user know what type of information is requested. Is it a number (what type of number)? Is it a string (such as the name of a country or a customer's name)? Is it the location of a file (such as C:\Program Files\Homework)? Are you expecting a Yes/No True/False type of answer (if so how should the user provide it)? Is it a date (if it is a date, what format is the user supposed to enter)? These questions can lead you to believe that you should state a clear request to the user and specify what kind of value you are expecting. For example, instead of the question above, you can implement the InputBox function as follows:

Private Sub cmdRequestDOB_Click ()
InputBox "Please enter your date of birth asmm/dd/yyyy"
End Sub

Another solution, also explicit enough, consists of providing an example to the user.

The second thing you should take care of is the value the user would have typed. After typing a value, the user would click one of the buttons: OK or Cancel. If the user clicks OK, you should retrieve the value the user would have typed. It is also your responsibility to find out whether the user typed a valid value. Because the **InputBox** () function can return any type of value, it has no mechanism of validating the user's entry. To retrieve the value of the Input Box dialog when the user clicks OK, you must use the **InputBox ()** function (and not the method as above). Here is anexample:

Private Sub cmdRequestDOB_Click ()
Dim dteDOB As Date

dteDOB = InputBox("Please enter your date of birth asmm/dd/yyyy")
txtDOB   =
dteDOB   End
Sub

Sometimes, even if you provide an explicit Input Box, the user might not provide a new value but click OK. The problem is that you would still need to get the value of the text box and you might want to involve it in an expression. You can solve this problem and that of providing an example to the user by filling the text box with a default value. Besides the prompt, Visual Basic provides a more elaborate InputBox function that allows you to specify more options, including a default value. The syntax used thenis:

InputBox (*prompt*, *Title*, *Default*, *XPos*, *YPos*, *HelpFile*, *Context*)

Using this syntax, you can provide a title to display on the title bar of the Input Box dialog. This is taken care of by the Title. The XPos and YPos arguments allow you decide the position of the Input Box from left (XPos) and top (YPos) measurements of thescreen.

Boolean Functions: IsEmpty

The **IsEmpty** function states that a field is empty. The syntax of the **IsEmpty** function is

IsEmpty (*Expression*)

In this case, the Expression argument will be set as empty. The **IsEmpty** function returns a Boolean value. The **IsEmpty** function is mostly used to check whether a field is empty. Then you would use the result for another purpose. The result in this case would be expressed as TRUE or FALSE.

Example =IsEmpty (MI)

This would result in the MI field being empty

Boolean Functions: IsNull

The **IsNull** function states an expression as being Null, which means the expression is set as a field that contains no value. The syntax of the **IsNull** function is

IsNull (*Expression*)

The **IsNull** function returns a Boolean value.

Properties of Forms, Reports, and Controls

Introduction

Users interact with your database by using forms and the controls those forms host. As a database developer, you create those forms and decide what controls are necessary to make your database a good product. To make the forms of your database as useful as possible, you should know what the various controls provide, which is primarily theirproperties.

A property is something that characterizes or describes an object. A property can be the name of an object, its color, the text it displays, or itswidth.

Controls Properties

When designing a form and manipulating <u>Windows controls</u>, you will use a central object called the Properties Window:

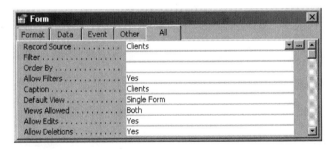

Made of five property sheets, the Properties window displays the properties associated with the object or the control that is selected on the form. To get the Properties window of the   properties associated with a control, right-click that control and clickProperties.

To display the Properties window for the form, double-click the button that is at the intersection of both rulers. You can also click the Properties button on the Form Design toolbar to toggle the Properties windows.

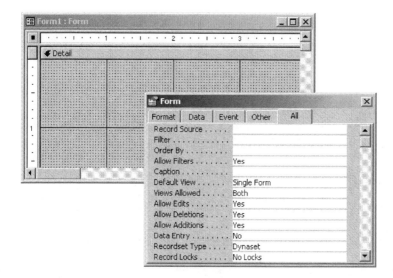

The properties of an object are divided in three main categories. Characteristics that control the form's appearance are listed in the **Format** property sheet. Characteristics that control internal or external relationships, as far as data is concerned, are listed in the **Data** property sheet. The **Other** property sheet lists characteristics that don't fit in one of the other groups. When dealing with a particular characteristic, you can access it from one of those property sheets or you can use the whole list of properties from the **All**propertysheet.

Practical Learning: Viewing the Form's Properties Window

1.   Open the **CPAP Help Desk1** database and click the Forms button or property sheet

2.   In the Forms section, Right-click Suppliers and click Design.

3.   To display the Properties window, double-click the button at the inter section of the rulers

. Notice that the Properties window displays 5 property sheets

4.   To switch the form to Form View, on the Form Design toolbar, click the View button.

5.   To close the form, click its close button.

Properties Categories

Properties are set by changing their values and there are various types of properties.

In the Properties window of Microsoft Access, a property is made of two parts: its name and its value:

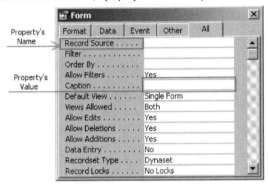

The name of a property displays on the left gray section. Although you can click it to select it, you cannot change it. The property name can be made of one word such as **Width**; it can also be made of a combination of words, such as **Record Source**. On this site, a property will be called by what displays on that left gray section. This means that, if a property displays "Height", we will call it "The Height Property". If it displays "Whats This Button", we will call it "The Whats This ButtonProperty".

In Visual Basic, the name of a property is made of one word starting in uppercase. Examples are **Text** or **Caption**. If the property is a combination of words, each component of the word would start in uppercase. Examples are **RecordSource** or **AllowAdditions**. Not all properties of the Microsoft Access' Properties window are exactly reproduced in Visual Basic but most of them are. And most of the properties have the same name, in oneword.

Before referring to a property in Visual Basic, you must first call the control whose property you want to use. There are various ways you can call a control. If you know the name of a control, you can type it and assign it default value. Here is an example:

```
Private   Sub   Form_Load  ()
txtFirstName
End Sub
```

Alternatively, you can let Visual Basic know that you are referring to an object that belongs to the same form in which the event is being written. In Visual Basic, a form refers to itself as **me**. In the Code Editor, after typing **me**, type the period operator. Visual Basic would display the list of properties and the controls that the form is hosting. This allows you to select the control or property you need. Using the me object, you can access acontrol:

Private   Sub
Form_Load   ()
txtFirstName
Me.txtLastName
End Sub

In the Properties window, the second part of a property displays on the right side of the property name. This is called the value of the property:

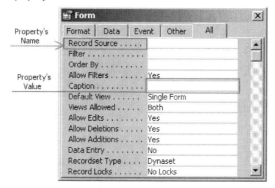

As properties are intended to fulfill different purposes, there are various categories of properties. In the Properties window, to give a value to a property, you type the desired value in the field on the right side of the name of you proceed as we will learn shortly, depending on the property type.

In Visual Basic, to change the value of a property, you can assign it the desired value, using the assignment operator

StringProperties

```
Record Source . . . . . . . . .  Employees
Filter . . . . . . . . . . . . . . . .
Order By . . . . . . . . . . . . .
```

In the Properties window, some properties display a word or a group of words. Such a word or group of words on a field is called a string. Some of those properties already display a value while some others are empty. To set or change such a string, you can click the property name and type the desired value, which would replace whatever text the property was displaying. Alternatively, you can edit the text that the property alreadyhas.

There are various types of string properties on the form and other controls. Examples include among others, the control's name or its caption.

To provide a string value to a property in Visual Basic, use the assignment operator and type the text in double-quotes. Here is an example:

```
Private Sub Form_Load ()
Me.Caption = "Visual Basic for Applications"
End Sub
```

String Properties: Controls Names

Everything that is every object, in your database needs a name (in fact, this includes every object used by the computer). A name allows the database engine (and the computer) to identify each object for any necessary reference. Although the name of a table (query, form, or report) doesn't appear as obvious as some other controls, as a property, it is highly valuable when creating expressions that involve the table (query, form, orreport).

There are two main ways an object (in this section, the word object includes not only the form but other Windows controls that we will be using during form and report designs) receives a name. If you create a form using the New Object button on the Table Datasheet toolbar, by default, Microsoft Access gives it the same name as the form (or the query) where its data originates from. Also, when you create a form using the Form Wizard, Microsoft Access would suggest the name of the source table (or query) to the form.

In these last two examples, you can accept the suggestedname.
Because a form and a table are two distinct objects, they can have the same name without any conflict. As an example, if you create a database using the Database Wizard, you would see that the tables and forms hold the same names.

The second option you have is to change the suggested name of the form. As we did with the tables, to set the name of a form, if it has not been previous saved (by you), you must ask to save the form and give the name you want. The name of a form follows the same rules we applied to tables. In this case, to identify a form as such, you can start its name with **from** followed by a word or group of words that can easily identify what the form is being used for.

1.   In the Forms section, right-click **Suppliers** and clickCopy

2.   Right-click an unoccupied area in the Forms section and clickPaste

3.   In the Paste As dialog box, type frmSuppliers and press Enter twice (the first Enter register the name, the second Enter opens theform).

String Properties: The Caption

The most upper characteristic that appear on a form is the word or group of words on the title bar. This is called the caption of the form and it is controlled by the Caption property. By default, the title bar displays the name of the form. To change this title, access the **Caption** field in the **Format** property sheet and type the desired title. Just like the caption of a table, the title of a form is not related to the form's name; therefore, you can type any caption you want, but a caption should reflect what the form is being usedfor.

Practical Learning: Setting the Form's Caption

1.   To switch the form to Design View, on the Form View tool bar, click the View button.

2.   To change the caption of the form, on the Properties window, click**Format**

3.   The cursor should be blinking in the Caption field; if not, click **Caption**.
Type **College Park Auto-Parts – Supplies Records**

4.   To view the caption, you must switch to Form View. On the menu bar, click View -> Form View.

5.   After viewing the caption, on the menu bar, click View -> Design View to switch the form to design mode.

Boolean Fields

```
Allow Filters . . . . . . . . . . .  Yes
Allow Edits . . . . . . . . . . . .  Yes
Allow Deletions . . . . . . . . .  Yes
Allow Additions . . . . . . . . .  Yes
Data Entry . . . . . . . . . . . .  No
```

Some fields behave like a True or False answer to a question. Such fields can display only one of two values. Both values come in a combo box that displays as the property field. There are three categories of these fields in combinations of Yes/No, True/False, or On/Off.

There are two main ways you use a Boolean field: either to set its value or to find out what value the field is holding. When studying conditional statements, we will learn the mechanics of finding out what value a property is holding. To change the value of the field in the Properties window, click the field to display its combo box. Then click the arrow of the combo box and select the othervalue.

To change the value of a Boolean field or variable in Visual Basic, assign it a True or False value, depending on your goals. Because the Code Editor would not display the list of possible values on the right side of the assignment operator, you can press Ctrl + Space to show the list.

From the list, you can select and double-click True or False. Of course, it is faster and easier to type the desired value since you already know what it should be.

If you are invoking a property of the Properties window, it is likely that Visual Basic is already aware that the property is Boolean. In that case, after typing the assignment operator, Visual Basic would display both True and False in a two-item list:

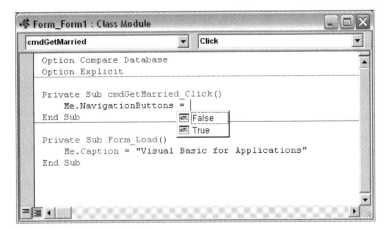

You can type t or f and press Tab (or Enter) to select the desiredvalue.

Navigating Buttons

When studying tables and during form's data entry, we found out that a form (also a table, a query, or a report) is equipped with some buttons on its lower section. These buttons allow the user to navigate back and forth through records. These buttons are very useful during data entry and data analysis. If you are creating a form that would display the same content all the time, such as a form that doesn't actually display records, you can hide the form navigationbuttons.

The presence or absence of navigation buttons is controlled by the Boolean **Navigation Buttons** property. When its value is set to **Yes**, the form would display the Navigation Buttons. To hide them, set the Navigation Buttons property value to**No**.

Practical Learning: Hiding the Navigation Buttons

1.   On the Form Design toolbar, click the Codebutton.

2.   In the Object combo box, click Form and implement its Load event asfollows:

```
Private      Sub      Form_Load      ()
Me.NavigationButtons =False
End Sub
```

3.   Return to the form and switch it to FormView.

4.   Notice that the form doesn't have the bottom navigation buttons. After using the form, switch it to Design View and get back to the Code Editor

Enumerated Properties

Picture Type	Embedded
Picture Size Mode	Clip
Picture Alignment	Center

A set is a list of words that composes the possible values of a property. The list, which is static, which means it cannot be changed, comes as a combo box where the user (in this case the user is the database developer) can select one item from. To change the property value in the Properties window, click the arrow of the combo box and select the desired value from thelist.

To set or change the value of an enumerated property in Visual Basic, you must know the value you want. There are two main alternatives: using your experience or getting help. If you know the possible values of the property, you can assign the desired value to the property name. If you don't know the possible values, you can get back to the Properties window, click the arrow of the combo box that is the property whose value you want to assign, view and write down the possible values. Here is anexample:

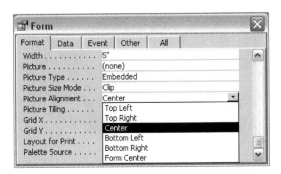

Once you have the list of possible values, you can get to the Code Editor and get ready to assign the desired value. Many of the values of properties from the Properties window are not exactly equivalent in Visual Basic. This means that you may not use the same values as in the Properties window. The help files can give you the list of possiblevalues.

Numeric Properties

Left	1.25"
Top	0.25"
Width	1.6042"
Height	0.1771"

Some properties use a value that is a number. There are two types of numbers you will be asked to provide, depending on the property. An integer is a number that doesn't take a decimal portion. Such a number can be made of digits only. For such a field, make sure you provide an integer of appropriate range, as you will possibly be directed to do. The other type of number will bedecimal.

A decimal number, also called a floating number, can be made of digits or a combination of digits and one period in between. When setting such a value, make sure that either you type only digits, or you type digits and one period; the period can be anywhere in the value, Microsoft Access would take care of formatting it if it judges itnecessary.

To change the value of a numeric property in the Properties window, you can click the property name to highlight the property value. Then you can type the desiredvalue.

To set the numeric value of a property is Visual Basic, use the assignment operator and assign the desired value to the property. Once again, the value must be a validnumber.

1.   In the Code Editor, change the Load event of the form asfollows:

```
Private      Sub      Form_Load      ()
Me.NavigationButtons  =  False  Width
= 4.128
End Sub
```

2.   Get back to the form and switch it to Form View to preview it. On the main menu, click Window
-> Size to FitForm

3.   Switch the form back to Design View.

Expressions Properties

```
Input Mask . . . . . . . . . . . .                    [...]
Default Value . . . . . . . . . .
Validation Rule . . . . . . . . .
```

Some properties display a value that is a more elaborate expression. If you know what value the property should display, namely an expression, you can just type it. Otherwise, Microsoft Access provides intermediary steps that you can follow to create or build the value. We will see examples of those when we study expressions and queries.

Using the From Wizard

The Form Wizard provides the easiest means of creating a form automatically. Like the objects wizards we had seen so far, this one also takes you step by step through creating the object.

There are two main ways you can launch the Form Wizard: from the Database Window or from the New Form dialog box. On the Database Window, click the Forms button. Then double-click Create Form by Using Wizard. On the New Form dialog box, click Form Wizard and click OK.

The first page of the Form Wizard allows you to choose the originating table or query that will supply the necessary fields in the form. Once you have selected the object, its corresponding fields display in the Available Fields list box, you can select all fields or decide which ones you want to include in the form.

The 2nd page of the wizard allows you to select the desired layout of the form. Forms can be designed in various flavors: Columnar, Datasheet, Tabular, Justified, or amix:

• A columnar form is used to display data one record at a time. This is a convenient display for data entry and analysis because the user is able to examine each piece of information for each onerecord:

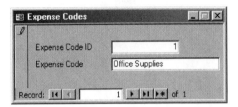

• A tabular form displays its data in a table layout following a continuous series of records. All or almost all records are displaying in a singlelayout:

There are three main ways you can create a tabular form: from the New Form dialog box, using the Form Wizard, or designing it.

• A datasheet form looks and behaves like a table, displaying all possible records at the same time instead of one record at atime:

A datasheet is mainly used in relationships to display another table's related records. It is also suitable for

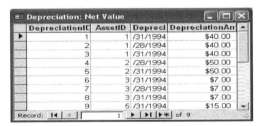

people who prefer to work in a spreadsheet environment. This display allows the database developer to provide a sheet view to the data entry personnel without making the table's design or formats available.

You can make the same form available in Form View and Datasheet View. In fact, most forms are. The users can switch from Form View to Datasheet View by clicking the View menu. Unfortunately, this could also allow the users to get the form in Design View, then they could modify it. If you don't want the users to have access to Design View but retain Form View and Datasheet View, you might have to create custom menus and toolbars.

There are two main ways you can create a Datasheet form: using the wizard or designing it.

• A Justified form provides a good and consistent look. When the form is created, borders are added tolabels:

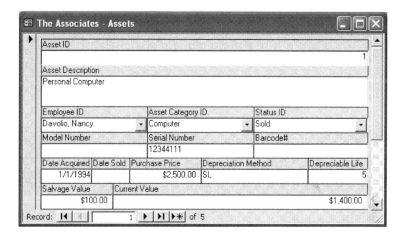

The 3rd page of the Form Wizard presents the forms designs you can choose from. These are the designs we saw when creating a database using the DatabaseWizard.

The 4th page allows you to name the form, using the naming convention we studied when creating the tables by providing an appropriate name.

Conditional Statements

Introduction

The essence of computer programming is on telling the computer what to do when something occurs, and how to do it. This is performed by setting conditions, examining them and stating what decisions the computer should make.

To perform the necessary conditions, you have two main options: Microsoft Access or Microsoft Visual Basic. Microsoft Access is equipped with a series of operators and functions destined to perform various operations. To use a condition in Microsoft Access, if you know the structure of the conditional statement, you can write it after typing an assignment operator. Because most conditions in Microsoft Access (namely IIf) are in the form of functions, we will study them later on. For now, we will learn how to write conditions in Visual Basic.

Microsoft Visual Basic comes with an lot of conditional statements for almost any situation your computer can encounter. As the application developer, it is up to you to anticipate these situations and make your program act accordingly.

A comparison is performed between two values of the same type; for example, you can compare two numbers, two characters, or the names of two cities. On the other hand, a comparison between two disparate values doesn't bear any meaning. For example, it is difficult to compare a telephone number and somebody's grand- mother name, or a music category and the distance between two points. Like the arithmetic operations, the comparison operations are performed on two values.

Unlike arithmetic operations where results are varied, a comparison produces only one of two results. The result can be an logical **True or False**.

To perform the necessary comparisons, Microsoft Access and Visual Basic use a series of logical operators and constants.

Logical Operators

The Comparison for E□uality =

To compare two variables for e□uality, use the = operator. Its syntax is:

Value1 = Value2

The e□uality operation is used to find out whether two variables (or one variable and a constant) hold the same value. From our syntax, the value of Value1 would be compared with the value of Value2. If Value1 and Value2 hold the same value, the comparison produces a True result. If they are different, the comparison renders **false or 0.**

The Logical Not Operator

When a variable is declared and receives a value (this could be done through initialization or a change of value) in a program, it becomes alive. When a variable is not being used or is not available for processing (in visual programming, it would be considered as disabled) to make a variable (temporarily) unusable, you can nullify its value. To render a variable unavailable during the evolution of a program, apply the logical not operator which is Not. Its syntax is:

Not Value

There are two main ways you can use the logical Not operator. As we will learn when studying conditional statements, the most classic way of using the logical not operator is to check the state of a variable.

When a variable holds a value, it is "alive". To make it not available, you can "not" it. When a variable has been "notted", its logical value has changed. If the logical value was true, it would be changed to False. Therefore, you can inverse the logical value of a variable by "notting" or not "notting" it.

For Inequality <>

As opposed to Equality, Visual Basic provides another operator used to compare two values for inequality, which is <>. Its syntax is:

Value1 <>Value2

The <> is a binary operator (like all logical operators except the logical **Not**, which is a unary operator) that is used to compare two values. The values can come from two variables as in Variable1 <> Variable2. Upon comparing the values, if both variables hold different values, the comparison produces a **True** value. Otherwise, the comparison renders **False** or a null value.

The inequality is obviously the opposite of the equality.

A Lower Value <

To find out whether one value is lower than another, use the < operator. Its syntax is:

Value1 <Value2

The value held by Value1 is compared to that of Value2. As it would be done with other operations, the comparison can be made between two variables, as in Variable1 < Variable2. If the value held by Variable1

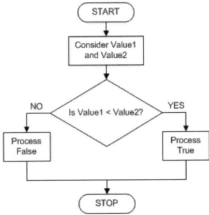

is lower than that of Variable2, the comparison produces a **True**.

Combining Equality and Lower Value <=

The previous two operations can be combined to compare two values. This allows you to know if two values are the same or if the first is less than the second. The operator used is <= and its syntax is:

Value1 <= Value2

The <= operation performs a comparison as any of the last two. If both Value1 and VBalue2 hold the same value, result is true or positive. If the left operand, in this case *Value1*, holds a value lower than the second operand, in this case *Value2*, the result is still true.

A Greater Value >

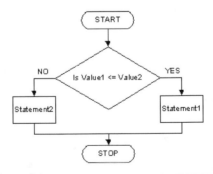

When two values of the same type are distinct, one of them is usually higher than the other. Visual Basic provides a logical operator that allows you to find out if one of two values is greater than the other. The operator used for this operation uses the > symbol. Its syntaxis:

Value1 > Value2

Both operands, in this case Value1 and Value2, can be variables or the left operand can be a variable while the right operand is a constant. If the value on the left ofthe

>operator is greater than the value on the right side or a constant, the comparison produces a **True** value. Otherwise, the comparison renders False or null.

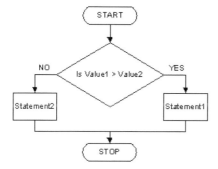

Greater or Equal Value >=

The greater than or the equality operators can be combined to produce an operator as follows: >=. This is the "greater than or equal to" operator. Its syntax is:

Value1 >= Value2

A comparison is performed on both operands: Value1 and Value2. If the value of Value1 and that of Value2

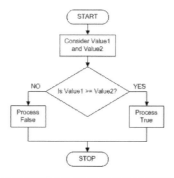

are the same, the comparison produces a **True** value. If the value of the left operand is greater than that of the right operand, the comparison still produces **True**. If the value of the left operand is strictly less than the value of the right operand, the comparison produces a **False**result.

Here is a summary table of the logical operators we have studied:

Operator	Meaning	Example	Opposite
=	Equality to	a = b	<>
<>	Not equal to	12 != 7	=
<	Less than	25 < 84	>=
<=	Less than or equal to	Cab <= Tab	>
>	Greater than	248 > 55	<=
>=	Greater than or equal to	Val1 >= Val2	<

The If...Then Statement

The If...Then statement examines the truthfulness of an expression. Structurally, its syntax is:

If *Condition* **Then** *Statement*

Therefore, the program will examine the *Condition*. This condition can be a simple expression or a combination of expressions. If the *Condition* is true, then the program will execute the *Statement*

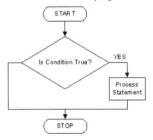

There are two ways you can use the **If...Then** statement. If the conditional expression is short enough, you can write it on one line using the followingsyntax:

If *Condition* Then *Statement*

In the following example, if the Gender text box of a form displays Male, the background color of the Detail section would be colored in light blue:

Private Sub Form_Current ()
If Gender = "Male" Then Detail.BackColor = 16772055
End Sub

If there are many statements to execute as a truthful result of the condition, you should write the statements on subsequent lines. Of course, you can use this technique even if the condition you are examining is short. If then you use the *Statement* on a different line, you must terminate the conditional statement with **End If**. The syntax used is:

If *Condition* Then
State
ment
End If

The example above can be re-written as follows:

Private Sub Form_Current ()
If Gender = "Male" Then
Detail.BackColor = 16772055
End If
End Sub

If the condition needs to cover many lines of code, the syntax to apply is:

If   *Condition*
Then
Statement1
Statement2

Statement_n
End If

Here is an example:

```
Private Sub Form_Current ()
If Gender = "Male" Then
Detail.BackColor = 16772055
FormHeader.BackColor = 16752478
FormFooter.BackColor = 14511872 End If
End Sub
```

The If...Then...Else Statement

The if...Then statement offers only one alternative: to act if the condition is true. Whenever you would like to apply an alternate expression in case the condition is false, use the **If...Then...Else** statement. The syntax of this statement is:

If *ConditionIsTrue* **Then**
Statement1
Else
Statement2
End If

The condition, in this *ConditionIsTrue*, would be examined. If it produces a true result, then the first statement, in this case *Statement1*, would be executed. If the condition (*ConditionIsTrue*) is false, the second statement, in this case *Statement2*, would be executed.

Here is an example:

```
Private Sub Form_Current ()
If Gender = "Male" Then
Detail.BackColor = 16772055
Else
Detail.BackColor = 13034239 End If
End Sub
```

If any of the expressions needs more than one line of code to have a complete implementation, you can include it in the needed section before the end of the section. Here is an example:

```
Private Sub Form_Current ()
If Gender = "Male" Then
Detail.BackColor = 16772055
FormHeader.BackColor =16752478
FormFooter.BackColor =14511872
Else

Detail.BackColor = 13034239
FormHeader.BackColor = 7452927
FormFooter.BackColor = 29670 End If
End Sub
```

The If...Then...ElseIf Statement

The If...Then...ElseIf statement acts like the **If...Then...Else**, except that it offers as many choices as necessary. The formula is:

If *Condition1* **Then**
Statement1
ElseIf *Condition2* **Then**
Statement2
ElseIf *Condition_n* **Then**
Stateme
nt_n
End If

The program will first examine the first condition, in this cases *Condition1*. If *Condition1* is true, then the program would execute the first statement, in this cases *Statment1*, and stop examining conditions. But if *Condition1* is false, then the program would examine *Condition2* and act accordingly. Whenever a condition is false, the program would continue examining the conditions until it finds one that is true. Once a true condition has been found and its statement executed, the program would terminate the conditional examination at End If.

The above syntax pre-supposes that at lease one of the conditions would produce a true result. Sometimes, regardless of how many conditions you use, it is possible that none of them would produce a true result. Therefore, in anticipation of such occurrence, you should provide an alternate statement that would embrace any condition that doesn't fit in the possible true results. This is done by combining an **If...Then...Else** and an **If...Then...ElseIf** statements. The resulting syntax to use is:

If *Condition1* **Then**
Statement1
ElseIf *Condition2* **Then**
Statement2
ElseIf *Condition3* **Then**
Statement3
Else
Statement_False
End If

In this case, if neither of the **If** and **ElseIf**s conditions was validated, then the last statement, in this case *Statement_False*, would execute.

The Select Case Statement

If you have a large number of conditions to examine, the **If...Then...Else** will go through each one of them, which could take long (although usually transparent to the user). Visual Basic offers an alternative of jumping to the statement that applies to the state of the condition. This is performed through the sue of the **Select Case** statement.

The syntax of the Select Case is:

Select Case *Expression*
Case
Expression1
Statement1
Case
Expression2
Statement2
Case
Expression_n

Statement_n
End Select

Visual Basic would examine the *Expression* and evaluate it once to get a general result. Then it would compare the result of *Expression* with the *Expressionn* of each case. Once it finds one that matches, it would execute the corresponding *Statements*.

Here is an example:

```
Private Sub cboMembership_After Update () Dim
strMembership As String
strMembership = [cboMembership].Text Select Case
strMembership
Case "Teen"
txtPrice = "$25" Case "Adult"
txtPrice = "$50" Case "Senior"
txtPrice = "$35" End Select
End Sub
```

If you anticipate that there could be no match between the *Expression* and one of the *Expressionn*, you can use a **Case Else** statement at the end of the list. The statement would then look like this:

Select Case *Expression*
Case
Expression1
Statement1
Case
Expression2

Statement2
Case
Expression3
Statement3
Case Else
Statement_n
End Select

Looping and Counting: Do...Loop

Loops are used to repeat an action. There are various variations of the **Do** loops. The syntax of the **Do While** loop is:

Do While *Condition*
Statement(s)
Loop

The program will first test the *Condition*. If the *Condition* is true, the program would execute the *Statement* or *Statement*s and go back to the **Do While** statement and test the condition again. This expression will execute the *Statement* or statements AS LONG AS the *Condition* is true, as many times as the *Condition* will be visited and found true. If the *Condition* is false, the program will skip the **Do While** statement and not executeany.

Since the **Do While** statement tests the *Condition* first before executing the *Statement*, sometimes you will want the program to execute the *Statement* first, then go back and test the *Condition*. Visual Basic offers a reverse to the syntax, which is:

Do
Statement(s)
Loop While *Condition*

In this case, Visual Basic will execute the *Statement* or *Statement*s first, then it will test the *Condition*. If the *Condition* is true, the program will execute the *Statement* again. The program will continue this examination-execution as long as the *Condition* is true. The big difference here is that even if the *Condition* is false, the program will have executed the *Condition* at least once.

An alternative to the **Do While** loop is the **Do Until**loop. Its syntax is:

Do Until *Condition*
Statement(s)
Loop

This loop will first examine the *Condition*, instead of examining whether the *Condition* is true, it will test whether the *Condition* is false.

The other side of the **Do Until** loop would execute the *Statement* first, then it would examine the *Condition*. The syntax used is:

Do
Statement(s)

Loop Until *Condition*

Counting and Looping: For...Next

If you don't know how many times a statement needs to be executed, you can use one of the **Do** loops. But whenever you want to control how many times a statement should be executed, the **for...Next** loop offers a better alternative. The syntax used is:

For *Counter* = *Start* To *End*
Statement(s)
Next

Used for counting, the **For...Next** loop begins counting at the *Start* point. Then it examines whether the current value (after starting to count) is greater than *End*; if that's the case, the program exits the loop. It then executes the *Statement* or *Statement*s. Next, it increments the value of *Counter* by 1 and examines the condition again. This process goes on until *Counter* = *End*.

The syntax above will increment the counting by 1 at the end of each statement. If you want to control how the incrementing processes, you can set your own, using the **Step** option. Here is the syntax you would use:

For *Counter* = *Start* To *End* Step *Increment Statement(s)*
Next *Counter*

You can set the incrementing value to your choice. If the value of *Increment* is positive, the *Counter* will be added its value. This means that you can give it a negative value, in which case the *Counter* would be subtracted the setvalue.

Counting and Looping: For...Each

Since the **For...Next** loop is used to execute a group of statements based on the current result of the loop counting from *Start* to *End*, an alternative is to state various steps in the loop and execute a group of statements for each one of the elements in the group. This is mostly used when dealing with a collection ofitems.

The syntax used is:

For Each *Element* in *Group*
Statement(s)
Next *Element*

The loop will execute the *Statement* or *Statement(s)* for each *Element* in the *Group*.

Fundamental Windows Controls

Introduction

To interact with the machine, the user of a computer uses objects called controls. The choice, appearance, and behavior of these controls is the responsibility of the application developer that you are. When creating an application, you should be aware of what your environment offers in terms of controls and what are the capabilities of those controls. Microsoft Access provides various controls you can use when designing your database application. If these controls are not enough, you can add some that ship with Visual Basic and sometimes you can purchase others from third-party vendors. To start, you should know what is already available in Microsoft Access and how you can expand over it.

The Form

The form is the most fundamental object of Microsoft Access and Visual Basic. It is a rectangular object whose main purpose is to host or carry other controls. This means that a form by itself is useless; it is the controls that it hosts that make its role significant on an application.

To create a form in Microsoft Access, if using Microsoft Access 97, open the New Form dialog box, select Design View and click OK. In Microsoft Access 2000 and 2002, a link on the Forms section of the Database Window, namely Create Form in Design View, allows you to jump to the Design View and create a form. The most basic thing to do is to save the form and voila, you have an form. We also know at this time that you can use the Form Wizard to easily create a completely configured form.

By default, the form you create in Microsoft Access is primarily used for data processing. For this reason, it is e□uipped with navigation buttons, an record selector bar and one or two dividing lines. A regular form in a Windows application doesn't need or use these three attributes. Therefore, if you don't need these visible traits on your form, you should set their Boolean properties to No.

Practical Learning: Creating a Form

1. Start Microsoft Access and open the **Bethesda Car Rental3**database.

2. On the Database Window, clickForms.

3. On the main menu, click Insert -> Form. In the Design Form dialog box, make sure nothing is selected in the Table or Query combo box and double-click DesignView

4.   To save the form, on the Form Design toolbar, click the Save button.

5.   Type Switchboard and pressEnter

Fundamental Properties of an Form

As you can see, a form is not a very interactive object, but it displays a few characteristics that would make it very valuable and allow it to provide a unique role.

As far as the user is concerned, on top, a form has a title bar made of three   sections. The system button on the left holds a menu that would allow the user to minimize, maximize, restore, move or close the form. On the right side of the   system button, the title displays a word or a group of words that we know as the caption. This same section of the title bar, which is the main section of the title bar, also is equipped with an menu that allows you or the user to perform some of the actions necessary for a database form. On the right side, the title bar displays system buttons that would allow the user to minimize, maximize, restore or close   the form. The characteristics of the title bar of an form are controlled by the following properties available from the Properties window of the form:

- The Control Box: When its Boolean property is set to Yes, the form can display the system icon on the left and the system buttons on the right. If you want neither the system icon nor the system buttons, you can set the Control Box property to No

- The Min Max Buttons: This is an enumerated property that controls the presence or not of the system buttons but it depends on the value of the Control Box property. If the Min-Max Buttons property is set to None and the Control Box is set to Yes, the form would display the system icon and the system Close button. The user would not be able to minimize, maximize, or restore the form but he or she can still close the form. If the Min Max Buttons property is set to None and the Control Box property is set to No, the form would display neither the system icon nor any of the system buttons. Consel uently, the user would not be able to close the form. This scenario can be used to control exactly how the form can be closed because, ultimately, you would have to provide a way for the user to close the form. The Min Max Buttons property also allows you to hide the maximize button with Min Enabled or to hide the minimize button with Max Enabled or to display all three system button with the Both Enabled value

- The Close Button: If the Control Box property is set to No, we saw that the Min Max Buttons property can control which system button, either minimize or maximize, would be available. Since the Min Max Buttons property has no bearing on the system Close button, you can use the Boolean Close Button property to decide whether the system Close button would be available to the user. The Close Button property doesn't show or hide the system Close button; it only enables or disables it.

If a form allows the user to close it, when the user closes an form, it fires an OnClose event. You can catch this to perform any necessary operation as a result of the form being closed.

The main area of the form can be referred to as its body. This is where the form would host other controls that would make the form useful. A form as a Windows object has distinguishable borders that make it resizable. This simply means that an user can widen, narrow, heighten, or shrink a form. The ability to resize a form is controlled by the Border Style property. For example, if you don't want the user to   be able to resize the form, you can set its Border Style property to Thin. If you don't want borders at all, you can set this property to none. This also removes the title bar, which consequently prevents the user from minimizing, maximizing, restoring, moving, or closing the form.

Practical Learning: Setting Form's Properties

1.　　UsingtheAllpropertysheetofthePropertieswindowfortheform,changeits**Caption**
To **Bethesda Car Rental**

2.　　Still using the Properties window for the form, set the **Record Selectors**,the
Navigation Buttons, and the **Dividing Lines** properties to **No**each

3.　　Set the **Border Style** property to**Thin**

4.　　Save the form and switch it to Form View to previewit

5.　　Click anywhere on the Database Window. Notice that the current form can be positioned
behind the DatabaseWindow

6.　　To bring the form back, on the main menu, click Window -> Bethesda Car Rental. Switch the
form back to DesignView

Form Design

As far as users are concerned, a form is a rectangular entity made for data Entry. Besides the form's characteristics that are visible to the user, behind the scenes, that is in Design View, a form can be made of three sections: the **Form Header**, the**Detail**, and the **Form Footer** sections. When all these three sections are not visible, if you need them, you can right-click anywhere on the form and click **Form Header/Footer**:

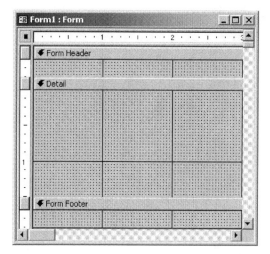

There is no perfect difference between these three sections. You can use (or not use) them as you wish. You can place any control on any section but it is traditional for data base developer stop lace all data entry control son the Detail section.

Remember that the user would never be aware of these sections unless you use some mechanism to make them visible.

Each one of these sections is mostly characterized by its height and its visual characteristics.

Practical Learning: Using Form's Sections

1.   Right-click in the form (under the Detail bar) and click **FormHeader/Footer**

2.   Double-click the **Form Header**bar.

3.   In the Properties window, click Height and type.**375**

4.   Double-click the **Form Footer** bar. On the Properties window, click Height and type.**3014**

5.   Switch the form to Form View to previewit

Dialog Boxes

A dialog box is a rectangular object that is used to host or carry other controls:

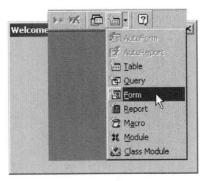

A dialog box is primarily characterized by two main features: its title bar and its body. The title bar, on top of the dialog box, has a title and the system close button. Although this is the classic appearance of a dialogbox, it is not strictly exclusive.

Some dialog boxes display the system icon. On the right side of the title bar, a classic dialog box displays only the system Close button made of X. Again, this is not exclusive. It is not unusual for a dialog box to display the minimize and the maximize/restore buttons.

To use a dialog box, the user must open it one way or another. Your job is to decide how and when the user will be able to open a dialog box.

To create a dialog box in Microsoft Access, you start from a form and display it in Design View. To convert an existing form into a dialog box, display it in Design View first.

There are two types of dialog boxes: modal and modeless.

Practical Learning: Creating a Modal Dialog Box

1.   To create a new form, on the (Form View) toolbar, click the arrow of the New Object button and click Insert ->Form

2.   On the New Form dialog box, double-click DesignView.

3.   Using your mouse, change the width of the form to **31/2** and change its height to**17/8**

4.   Save the form asdlgAboutBCR

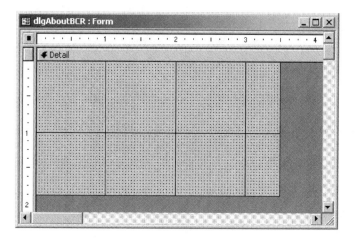

dal Dialog Boxes

A dialog box is characterized as modal if the user must close it before continuing with another task on the same application.

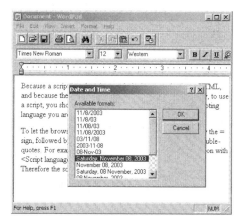

The Date and Time dialog box of WordPad is an example of a modal dialog box: if opened, the user must close it in order to continue using WordPad.

In order to use a dialog box in your application, your first decision would be on why you want a dialog box. This means that you should analyze a scenario and define if the dialog box is necessary. Use a dialog box if you want the user to first terminate whatever task she would be performing. For example, if a user is performing a payment of an order processing, it is natural for the user to process and finish that payment before starting another task.

To create a modal dialog box in Microsoft Access, start a form in Design View and set its **Border Style** property value to **Dialog**. Unfortunately, as far as Windows is concerned, this only reduces the system buttons to the Close button only. A classic (or normal) dialog box would need neither a **Record Selectors** bar nor the record navigation buttons. Therefore, you should decide how the dialog box would be used. If you want a regular dialog box as those available on non-database applications, you should set the **Record Selectors**, the **Navigation Buttons** and the **Dividing Lines** properties to **No** each.

Practical Learning: Creating a Modal Dialog Box

1. On the Properties window, change the Caption property to About the Bethesda Car RentalApplication

2. Change the **Record Selectors**, the **Navigation Buttons**, and the **Dividing Lines** properties to**No**

3. Change the **Modal** property to**Yes**

4. Change the **Border Style** property to**Dialog**

5. Save and preview the dialog box. When previewing the dialog box, on the main menu, click Window -> Size to FitForm.

6. After viewing the dialog box, close it, using its Close button

7. Press F11 to display the Database Window. Click Forms to display the Forms section or the Forms propertysheet

8. Right-click **About BCR** and clickRename.

9. Press Home, type **dlg** and press Enter. This changes the name of the dialog box to**dlgAboutBCR**.

Modeless Dialog Boxes

A dialog box is referred to as modeless if the user doesn't have to close it in order to continue using the application that owns the dialog box:

The Find dialog box of WordPad (also the Find dialog box of most applications) is an example of a modeless dialog box. If it is opened, the user doesn't have to close in order to use the application or the document in the background.

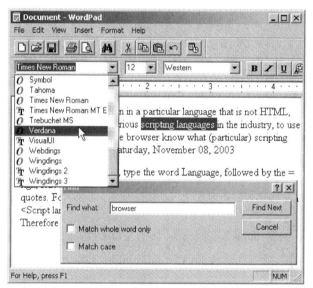

Since the modeless dialog box doesn't display its button on the task bar, the user should know that the dialog box is opened. To make the presence of a modeless dialog box obvious to the user, it typically displays on top of its host application until the user closesit.

To create a modeless dialog box, or to convert a form into a modeless dialog box, when in Design View, set the **Popup** property to **Yes**. This makes sure that the user can work on another form and the modeless dialog box or form would remain on top of any other form of yourdatabase.

Practical Learning: Creating a Modal Dialog Box

1. To create a new form, in the Forms section of the DatabaseWindow, click New.

2. On the New Form dialog box, double-click DesignView

3. Save the form as**dlgRentalRates**

4. On the Properties window, change the Caption to **Bethesda Car Rental - RentalRates**

5. To make the form a modeless dialog box, set the **Record Selectors**,the **Navigation Buttons**, and the **Dividing Lines** properties to **No**

6. Set the **Pop Up** property to**Yes**

7. Set the **Min Max Buttons** property to**None**

8. Switch the dialog box to FormView.

9. Click any area of the Database Window. Notice that the modeless dialog box stays ontop

10. Close the dialog box. When asked whether you want to save the form,click Yes

Controls: The Label

A label is a control used to display text on a form or dialog box. This control is for one of two main purposes: to provide quick information or to help the user identify another control on the form. In the strict sense, a label is usually not considered a Windows control. This is probably because the user has no other interaction with a label than to read the text the label displays. Therefore, the properties of a label are completely under your control: the user cannot change them (unless indirectly, that is under yourcontrol).

To create a label, on the Toolbox, click the **Label** button, click on the form or dialog box in Design View and type the desired text. After typing the text, you can control the properties of the label visually or using the Properties window.

Practical Learning: Creating a Modal Dialog Box

1. With the dlgAboutBCR form still open, to bring it up, on the main menu, click Window

-> Bethesda Car Rental. Switch the form to DesignView

2. If the Toolbox is not displaying, on the main menu, click View ->Toolbox.
On the Toolbox, click Label and click on the top-left section of the form (under the Detail bar)

3. Type Bethesda Car Rental(r)

4. On the Toolbox, click Label and click under the first label. Type Release2.02

5. Add another label with the caption This product is licensedto

6. Add another label with the caption Bethesda CarRental

7. Add another label with the caption A Division of BCR Productions, Inc.

8. Complete the dialog box and its labels as follows:

9. Save theform

Windows Controls: The Text Box

A text box is used to receive information from the user by her typing it into a rectangular box. A text box can also be used to simply display information to the user.

Although a text box is a good control by itself, it usually doesn't mean much to the user if she doesn't know what the box is used for. Therefore, you should always create a text box in conjunction with a label. The label is used to identify what the text box is used for. You should position the label on the left or on top of the text box. The rules of using the computer suggest that a text box be identified by the caption of its label. For example, if an label displays First Name, the text box on its right or under it would be called The First Name Text Box. If a label displays How Old Are You? Its corresponding text box would be called The How Old Are You Text Box. But, programmatically, the text box and its label are completely independent, in their behavior, functionality, and properties.

Practical Learning: Creating a Modal Dialog Box

1. Heighten (make tall) the Form Footer section so it would have a height of 1" On the main menu, click View -> FormHeader/Footer.
On the Toolbox, click the Text Box button.

2. On the form, click under the Form Footer bar. Click the accompanying label to select it and pressDelete.

3. Using the Properties window, move the text box the left and, using the Properties window, change its name totxtWarning

4. Change the Back Color to 14869218 (Red = Green = Blue =226)

5. Set the Special Effect to Shadowed and resize the text box asfollows:

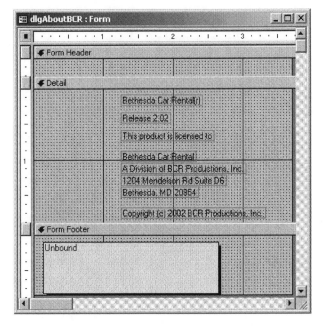

6. On the Form Design toolbar, click theCodebutton On the Objectcombo box, selectForm.

7. Implement the form's OnLoad event asfollows:

Private Sub Form_Load ()

Dim strWarning As String

Str Warning = "Unauthorized reproduction or distribution" & _ "of this program, any of its

objects, code " & _ "sections, or any of its portions, may result " & _ "in severe civil and criminal penalties. Such " &_

"activity will be prosecuted to the full extent " & _ "possible of the applicable law."

txtWarning = strWarning txtWarning.Enabled = False

txtWarning.Locked = True

End Sub

8.   Save the form and previewit

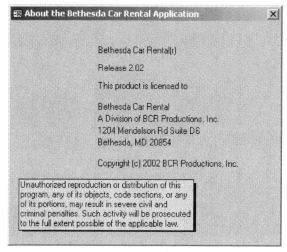

9.   Close the form and close MicrosoftAccess

Practical Learning: Adding an Unbound Picture

1.   Switch the form back to Design View and reduce the height of the header section to0

2.   On the Toolbox, click Unbound ObjectFrame

3.   On the form, click on the left side under the Detailbar

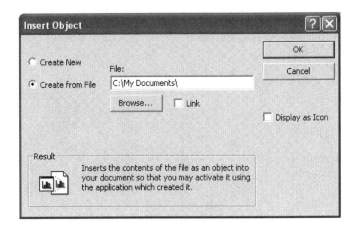

4. On the Insert Object dialog box, click the Create From File radio button and click the Browse...button

5. Locate and select bcrlogo1 and clickOpen

6. On the Insert Object dialog box, clickOK

7. On the form, make sure the new picture is selected. On the Properties window set the Size Mode toStretch

8. Set the Special Effect property to Flat and preview theform

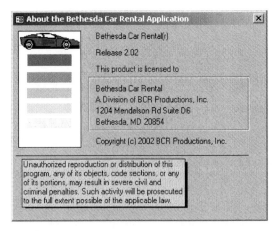

---

9. Save and close the dialog box

Relations-Based Controls

Introduction

One of the main and most valuable features of are national data base is the ability for objects to exchange information. This ensures that data is uniquely identified and not duplicated among the various objects of the application. Information entered on a form during data entry is made available to other forms and reports that would need it. This behavior and its related functionalities are configured and controlled through the relationships that various objects have towards eachother.

Practical Learning: Starting the Application

1. Start Microsoft Access and open the **Bethesda Car Rental3** database.Click Forms if necessary

2. Double-click the frmCars form to open it. Notice that we don't know who create this record although this information can be valuable during in venture

3. After viewing the form, close it.

The Fundamentals of Relational Database

Imagine you are a high school teacher. Every month you give homework to your students. After they have done their homework, you need to enter their grades in a database. If you have 40 to 200 students, it wouldn't make sense to create a new record for each student every time you need to enter his grades into the database. A relational database allow the student administrator to create students records, that is, their personal information in a designated object (a form). When a teacher wants to enter grades for a particular student, he can open the appropriate form.

This teacher should be able to select a select on the grade for instead of creating a new student. This also prevents duplicate information: if different teachers create a new record for each student, the student would end up with various records with possible different if not contradictory data.

To manage the flow of data from a table A to a table B, table B should have a field, like an ambassador, that represents the records of table A. Based on this, when somebody is processing any type of information on table B but needs information that is stored in table A, a control should allow the user to select, from table B, the information stored in table A without explicitly opening table A. To create such a scenario and relationship, the "ambassador" field of table B must have the same data type as the primary key of table A.

Practical Learning: Starting the Application

1.   On the Data base Window, click Tables and double-click tblCars to open the table in Data sheet View

2.   After viewing the table, switch it to Design View.

3.   Right-clickNbr Of Doors and click Insert Rows. Type **Car CategoryID** and press Tab

4.   Set the **Data Type** as **Number** and pressF6

5.   In the lower section of the table, accept **Long Integer** as the **Field Size**. Change the **Caption** to **Category** and delete the 0 of Default Value

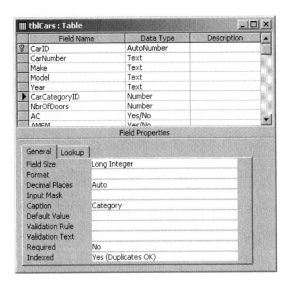

6.   Right-click Car Number and click Build

7.   In the Field Builder dialog box, in the Sample Tables, click Employees. In the Sample Fields, click EmployeeID and clickOK

8.   In the lower section of the table, change the Caption to Registered By

9.   Right-click AC and click Insert Rows. Type TransmissionID

10.   Change its Data Type to Number and make sure its Field Size is set to Long Integer. Setits Captionto Transmission and delete the 0 of the Default Value field

11.   Save and close thetable

Configuring Relationships

We have previously added fields to a table so the table can receive some of its data from other table. The only thing we did was to create fields, the table is still not aware of the other tables. We want to make sure that, if data is deleted on the table that holds the information, the dependent table must be made aware and dismiss the data that the originating table was providing. On the other hand, if data from the originating table changes, for example, if the name of an employee gets changed or updated in the Employees table, the change must be transparently updated on the newtable.

Practical Learning: Making a Form Active

1.   On the main menu, click Tools->Relationships...

2.   Right-click in the Relationships window and click Show Table. In the Show Table dialog box, click tblEmployees and click Add

3.   Double-click tblCars, tblCar Categories, and tblCar Transmissions

4.   Click Close.
If you ever want to re-position a table, click and drag its title bar to the desired location.

5.   On the tblEmployees table, click and drag EmployeeID. Drop it on top of EmployeeID in the tblCarstable:

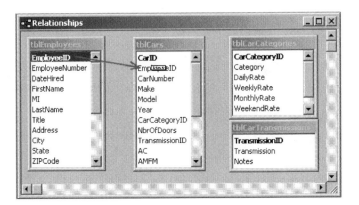

6. When the Relationships dialog box comes up, click the Enforce Referential Integrity check box and click the other two check boxes that would allow an update or a deletion of an employee from the tblEmployees table to be replicated in the tblCarstable

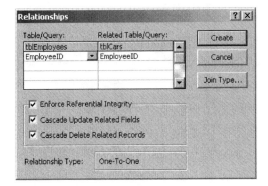

7. ClickCreate.

8. From the tblCar Categories table, drag Car CategoryID and drop it on top of Car CategoryID in the tblCars table

9. On the Relationships dialog box, click all three check boxes and click JoinType

10.   In the Join Properties dialog box, click the 2 radio button to ensure the data base that one category from the tblCar Categories table can be applied to various cars in the tblCarstable

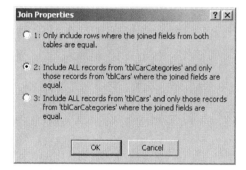

11.   Click OK and click Create.

12.   Right-click the line that joins both Employee IDs and click Edit Relationship. Click Join Type and click the 2 radio button

13.   Click OK twice

14.   Drag Transmission ID from the tblCar Transmissions table to the Transmission ID of the tblCars table. Enforce both referential integrities and ensure that one transmission from the tblCar Transmissions table can be applied to valious records of the tblCars table

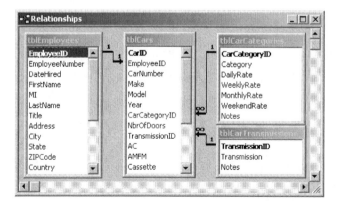

15. Close the Relationship window. When asked whether you want to save it, click

Yes

List-Based Controls: The Combo Box

Besides the table that is at the core of a database, the operating system provides an few controls that are more adapted to display a list of items. One of these controls is the combo box.

A combo box is a window control that presents a list of items the user can select from. Visually, a combo box looks like a text box e□uipped with a down pointing arrow on its right side. By default, a combo box displays an item. In order to change the content of that box, different options are available. You can allow the user to type in the combo box and try to match what the user types with one of the items in the list. You can also make the user only select an item from the list by clicking the down pointing arrow. If the list is long and cannot display everything at the same time, a combo box is e□uipped with a vertical scroll bar.

There are two main types of combo boxes you will provide to your users. A classic combo box that is popular on regular applications displays a list of items.You create such a list and know its content all the time.Such a combo box is not bound to anything else.This is called an unbound combo box.

An unbound combo box can be created on a table, a form, or an report. To create an unbound combo box, if the table is displaying in Datasheet View, you can right-click a column and click Lookup Column... If the table is displaying in Design View, choose the Lookup Wizard as the Data Type for the desired field. In both cases a Lookup Wizard dialog box would come up and guide you

To create an unbound combo box for an form or report, open the object in Design View. On the Toolbox, click Combo Box and click on the form or report. If the Control Wizard button was selected in the Toolbox, in both cases a Combo Box Wizard would come up and guide you.

Practical Learning: Creating an Unbound Combo Box

1. On the Database Window, click Tables. Right-click **tblTSDoubleShift** and click Design

2. Right-click **Tuesday In** and click Insert-Rows. Type **MondayIn2** and press Tab.

3. For the Data Type, select Lookup Wizard...

4. In the first page of the Lookup Wizard, click the second radio button and click Next

5.   Click under Col1 and type 09:00AM

6.   Press the down arrow key and type 12:00PM

7.   Press the down arrow key and type 12:30PM

8.   Press Tab and type 05:00PM

9.   Click Next and click Finish

10.   Save and close the table

11.   On the Data base Window, click **Forms** and double-click **from TS Double Shift1** to open it:

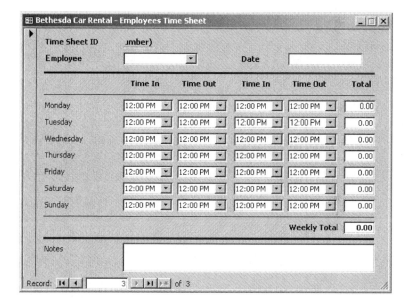

12.   Switch it to Design View. On the Form Design toolbar, click the Code button

13.   The first thing we are going to do is to calculate the time an employee has worked for one day. Our time sheet is designed with two shifts for each day. There are two possible scenarios: an employee can work two shifts in one day or an employee can take a (too long) (lunch) break. We will divide the responsibility on the database developer and the user. As the developer, you will take care of checking and validating the times

sequences. The user will have to make sure that, he did not take a break, he has to make sure that this reflects on the time sheet. If he puts a time a break between both shifts, the total time would subtract such an interception.

We will use a function that can receive the four time values of a date and calculate the total time worked for the day. In the Code Editor, type the following function:

```
Private Function Calc Today Time(TimeIn1 As Date, TimeOut1 As Date,_
TimeIn2 As Date, TimeOut2 As Date) AsDouble ' This variable will hold the time difference for the
firstshift
Dim dblShift1 As Double
'                  This variable will hold the time difference for these cond shift Dim dbl Shift2
AsDouble

dblShift1 = DateDiff("n", TimeIn1, TimeOut1) /60 dblShift2 =
DateDiff("n", TimeIn2, TimeOut2) /60

'                  The time worked is the total of bothshifts Calc
Today Time = dblShift1 +dblShift2
End Function
```

14.   Once we can get the total for each day, we can retrieve the value displayed for each day and calculate the total time for the week. To get this total, type the following procedure:

```
Private Sub Calculate Total Time ()
'                  This function is used to calculate the total time
'                  Based on the time displayed in the text box for each day Dim
Monday AsDouble
Dim Tuesday As Double Dim
Wednesday AsDouble  Dim
Thursday  As  Double  Dim
Friday  As  Double  Dim
Saturday  As  Double  Dim
Sunday As Double Dim Total
AsDouble

'                  Get the number of hours that isdisplaying ' in
each  text  box  of  the  corresponding  day  Monday
=CDbl(txtMonday)
```

```
Tuesday  =  CDbl(txtTuesday)  Wednesday
=CDbl(txtWednesday)       Thursday       =
CDbl(txtThursday)       Friday       =
CDbl(txtFriday)       Saturday       =
CDbl(txtSaturday)       Sunday       =
CDbl(txtSunday)

'              Calculate the total number of hours for theweek Total
= Monday + Tuesday + Wednesday +_
Thursday + Friday + Saturday + Sunday

'              Put the total in the Weekly Hours textbox
txtWeeklyTotal =Total
End Sub
```

15.   Now we are ready to calculate to the actual time for each day. First, we must validate the time values that the user selects on a combo box, depending on the combo box. Consider a day like Monday. The starting time that the user selects should not be higher than the end time. This means that a user cannot state that he worked from 12PM to 9AM in one day. Logically, such as sequence doesn't make sense. Therefore, the first time in for Monday must not occur after the first time out for Monday.

To implement this algorithm, in the Object combo box, select **MondayIn1** and, in the Procedure combo box, select **After Update**.

16.   Implement the **After Update** event as follows:

```
Private  SubMondayIn1_After  Update  ()
Dim InSel1 As Date
Dim OutSel1 As Date Dim
InSel2   As   Date   Dim
OutSel2 As Date

'              Get the time combo boxes that are involved on this After Update In Sel1
=CDate(MondayIn1)
OutSel1 = CDate(MondayOut1)

'              If the user has After Updated the time on MondayIn1, 'make
```

sure the new time doesn't occur after Monday Out 1

'   If the user tries this, set Monday In1 to the value of Monday Out1 If Out Sel1 <

InSel1Then

MondayIn1 = MondayOut1 End If

'   Get the current selections in the combo boxes for this day ' Convert

their values to date

InSel1 = CDate (MondayIn1) Out Sel1

=   CDate(MondayOut1)   InSel2   =

CDate(MondayIn2)   OutSel2   =

CDate(MondayOut2)

'   Send the time values the Calc Today Time function for processing txt

Monday = Calc Today Time(InSel1, OutSel1, InSel2,OutSel2)

'   Call the Calculate Total Time procedure to display the total time Calculate

Total Time

End Sub

17.   When it comes to the first time out value, we need to fulfill two conditions: a) the value of the first

time out must not be lower than that of the first time in; b) the value of the first timeout must not be higher

than that of the second time in.

To implement this behavior, on the Object combo box, select **MondayOut1** and, in the Procedure

combo box, select **After Update**.

Command Controls

Introduction

In the world of Microsoft Windows operating systems, a button is an object that a user clicks either in response to a question or to initiate an action. In Microsoft Access, there are three main types of buttons: the option button, the check box, and the command button.

Window Controls: The Radio Buttons

Also referred to as a radio button, an option button is a Windows control made of two sections: a round box O and a label. The label informs the user as to what the control is used for. The user makes her decision by selecting or clicking the round box 8. In practical usage, a radio button is accompanied by one or more other radio buttons that appear and behave as a group. The user decides which button is valid by selecting only one of them. When the user clicks one button, its round box fills with a (big) dot: 8. When one button in the group is selected, the other round buttons of the (same) group are emptied. The user can select another button by clicking a different choice, which empties the previous selection. This technique of selecting is referred to as mutually-exclusive.

Because they behave as a group, radio buttons are created using another object that can "hold" or host them. In Microsoft Access, this is usually accomplished by the presence of a Group Box object.

Practical Learning: Creating Option Buttons

1.   Start Microsoft Access and create a Blank Database named Computer Store

2.   On the main menu, click Insert -> Table. On the New Table dialog box, double- click Design View

3.   Type the first field as Order Processing ID

4.   Change its Data Type to AutoNumber and make it the Primary Key of the table

5.   Set the name of the second field as Monitor and press Tab

6.   For its Data Type, select Look up Wizard...

7. On the first page of the Lookup Wizard, click the second radio button and click Next

8. Click the empty field under Col1 and Type Monitor1

9. Press Tab, type Monitor2 and complete the list as follows:

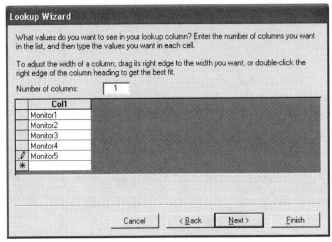

10. Click Next

11. Accept the label as Monitor and click Finish

12. Close the table. When asked whether you want to save it, clickYes.

13. Type **tblOrders** and pressEnter.

14. On the main menu, click Insert -> Form. On the New Form dialog box, click Design View. On the table or query combo box, select tblOrders and clickOK

15. On the Toolbox, click Text Box and click on the top left section of theform.

16. Change the label to Order ID and, on the Properties window, change the

Control Source of the text box to Monitor

17.   On the Toolbox, make sure the Control Wizards button is down and click Option Group

18.   Click on the form.

19.   When the first page of the Option Group Wizard displays, click the empty box under Label Names and type 15 Inch Color

20.   Press Tab and complete the list as follows:

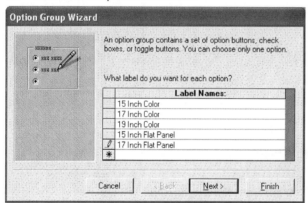

21.   Click Next.

22.   On the second page of the wizard, leave the first option as default and click next.

23.   On the third page, accept the suggested structure of the list and click next.

24.   On the fourth page, click the arrow of the combo box and select Monitor

25. Click Next

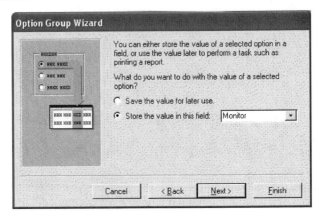

26. On the fifth page, accept the suggested layout and click Next

27. On the sixth page, change the label to Monitor and click Finish

28. Save the form as frm Orders and preview it

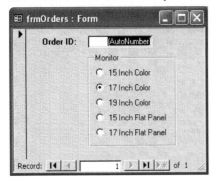

29. Close the form

Windows Controls: Check Boxes

A check box is a control that allows the user to validate or invalidate an option. Although it can appear by itself, a checkbox sometimes comes in a group with others, allowing the user to select as many choices as are available. Depending on the compiler or the environment, a little square appears with a checkbox S and a label. The user makes her selection by clicking in the square which toggles a check mark ☐. Toggling means if the square were empty ☐, after clicking it, a check mark would appear in it S; otherwise, the check mark would be removed.

From the user's standpoint, a checkbox is selected when its check mark is set; and the item is not selected when its square is empty.

From the developer standpoint, a check mark has two (Boolean) values: true or false (or TRUE or FALSE, or True or False). When a check mark is selected, its value is true; otherwise, its value is false. Those are the primary concerns you will have with check marks.

A check mark is a special button and can be programmed with a regular button. Therefore, depending on your needs, you can display or hide it at will; you can enable and disable it as necessary; you can adjust its behavior depending on other controls on the same form or the same application.

Check boxes provide a non-exclusive choice, which means each can behave as independent as you want with regard to the other check boxes of the same group. Therefore, although not recommended, you can create checkboxes anywhere on the form or report. If you plan to use a group of checkboxes, it is recommended that you include them in a rectangular container so their belonging to the same group will be obvious to the user. The group can be hosted by a **Group Box** (recommended) or a rectangle.

To create a checkbox in Microsoft Access, if the checkbox will be tied to a value on a table, set the Data Type of the field to Yes/No.

Practical Learning: Creating Check Boxes

1. Open the **tblOrders** table in Design View

2. Click the first empty field under Monitor and type **Has Power Cord**

3. Set its Data Type to Yes

4. Save and close the table

5. Open the **frmOrders** in Design View

6. Display the Field List window.

Drag **Has Power Cord** from the Field List and drop it on the form.

7. Change its label to **Has Power Cord?** and position it as follows:

8. Save and close the form

9. Open the Ocean Service Computer Store database and open the frm Order Processing form

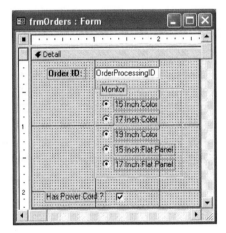

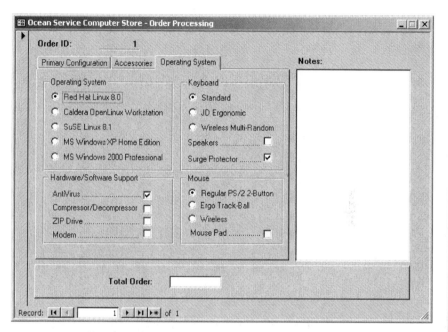

10. After viewing the form, switch it to Design View

11. On the Form Design toolbar, click the Code button 🔳

12. Instead of performing a calculation for each control on the form, we will use a central procedure that can take care of all calculations. Therefore, in the Code Editor, type the following procedure

```
Public Sub Calculate Order ()
Dim    curProcessor    As
Currency Dim  curHardDrive
As  Currency  Dim  curRAM
AsCurrency
Dim    curRemovable    As
Currency Dim curMonitor As
```

Currency Dim curNIC

13. Now, every time the user makes a selection, we will call the central procedure to update its calculation. To achieve this, at the end of the previous procedure, enter the following (Normally, you should select a control in the Object combo box and, in the Procedure combo box, select After Update for a Group Box. The Click event should be selected by default for a check box. After selecting the event, call the above procedure. At the end, the event should look as follows (the result is the same if you simply type the following code):

Private Sub Anti-Virus _
Click () Calculate Order
End Sub

14. Close the Code Editor and preview the form

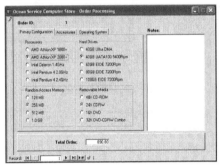

Save and close the form

Windows Controls: The Command Buttons

A button, sometimes referred to as a command button, is a rectangular object that allows the user to dismiss a dialog box or to initiate and action. This is done through a decision making process based on what a form or a dialog box is displaying. This could be an acknowledgement such as a form displaying a simple message to the user. A user could also be asked to choose one button from a group of buttons on a form or a dialog box. *To use* a button, the user positions her mouse pointer on the desired button and presses the left button. This action is referred to as clicking. Depending on how the button is implemented, it should be obvious to the user what to do with the button. A button can display a word or a group of words on its top.

This word or group of words is referred to as the button's caption. The caption should be explicit enough to let the user know what the button is used for. A caption like OK usually means the user accepts what message the form or dialog box is displaying. A caption like Cancel is usually accompanied by another OK button on the form. When a button has a Cancel button, the user would usually click it as if saying, "Never Mind" or "I change my mind", etc.

Normally, to create a command button, you click the Command Button on the Toolbox and click on the desired section of the form. On the Toolbox, if the Control Wizards button was down or clicked, a wizard would start to help you create a fully functional button. If you don't want to use the wizard, you click Cancel on the first page of the Command Button Wizard. Also, if you don't want to use the wizard, on the Toolbox, you can click the Control Wizards button to have it up.

Microsoft Access, filled with limitless wizards, has greatly simplified the creation of command buttons. This is done using the Command Button Wizard. This wizard can help you configure almost any kind of behavior that a button is supposed to implement a database application.

Practical Learning: Creating Command Buttons

1.   Open the **Bethesda Car Rental3** database and click the Forms button on the Database Window

2.   Double-click dlgAboutBCR to open

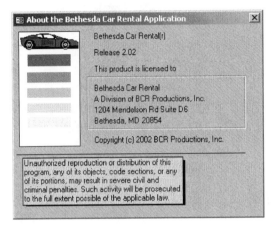

3. To switch it to Design View, right-click its title bar and click Form Design

4. On the Toolbox, make sure the Control Wizards button is selected 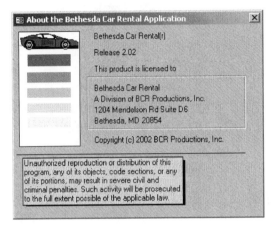. Click the Command Button

5. On the form, click under the Form Footer bar and on the right side of the Unbound text box

6. On the first page of the Command Button Wizard, in the Categories list, click Form Operations

7. In the Actions list, click Close Form

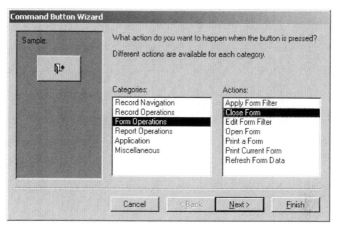

Click Next

8. On the second page, replace the content of the Text text box with OK (and make sure the Text radio button has been selected) and click Next

9. Change the name of the button to cmdClose and click Finish

10. Resize the button as follows:

11. Preview the dialog box:

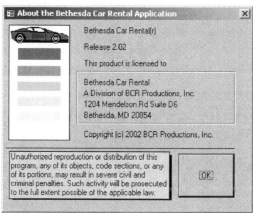

12. Save the form. To close the it, click OK. Also close Microsoft Access

Disclaimer

Disclaimer All the material contained in this book is provided for educational and informational purposes only. No responsibility can be taken for any results or outcomes resulting from the use of this material. A while every attempt has been made to provide information that is both accurate and effective, the author does not assume any responsibility for the accuracy or use/misuse of this information.

Other Books By (Andrei Besedin)

1) **50 Most Powerful Excel Functions and Formulas: Advanced Ways to Save Your Time and Make Complex Analysis Quick and Easy!** https://www.amazon.com/Most-Powerful-Excel-Functions-Formulas/dp/1521549915/ref=zg_bs_132559011_7?_encoding=UTF8&psc=1&refRID=QT5D1NR6CBRAFTGEP7AG

2) **SECRETS OF LOOKUP: BECOME MORE PRODUCTIVE WITH VLOOKUP, FREE YOUR TIME!** https://www.amazon.com/SECRETS-LOOKUP-PRODUCTIVE-VLOOKUP-Training-ebook/dp/B073P4FVSG/ref=la_B07211P1NS_1_10?s=books&ie=UTF8&qid=1499524730&sr=1-10

3) **Top 3 Excel Formulas and Functions** https://www.amazon.com/Excel-Formulas-Functions-Training-Book-ebook/dp/B0738LF8LL/ref=sr_1_6?ie=UTF8&qid=1499524945&sr=8-6&keywords=top+3+excel

4) **Amazing JAVA: Learn JAVA Quickly!** https://www.amazon.com/Amazing-JAVA-Learn-Quickly-ebook/dp/B0737762M8/ref=la_B07211P1NS_1_2?s=books&ie=UTF8&qid=1499524891&sr=1-2&refinements=p_82%3AB07211P1NS

5) **Dash Diet to Make Middle Aged People Healthy and Fit: 40 Delicious Recipes for People Over 40 Years Old!** https://www.amazon.com/Dash-Diet-Middle-People-Healthy-ebook/dp/B071WZBZPB/ref=la_B07211P1NS_1_3?s=books&ie=UTF8&qid=1499524891&sr=1-3&refinements=p_82%3AB07211P1NS

6) **Mediterranean diet for middle aged people: 40 delicious recipes to make people over 40 years old healthy and fit!** https://www.amazon.com/Mediterranean-diet-middle-aged-people-ebook/dp/B0723952FH/ref=la_B07211P1NS_1_4?s=books&ie=UTF8&qid=1499524891&sr=1-4&refinements=p_82%3AB07211P1NS

7) **Fitness for Middle Aged People: 40 Powerful Exercises to Make People over 40 Years Old Healthy and Fit!** https://www.amazon.com/Fitness-Middle-Aged-People-Exercises-ebook/dp/B072VFBT99/ref=la_B07211P1NS_1_5?s=books&ie=UTF8&qid=1499524891&sr=1-5&refinements=p_82%3AB07211P1NS

8) **Market Research: Global Market for Germanium and Germanium Products** https://www.amazon.com/Market-Research-Global-Germanium-Products-ebook/dp/B00X4JBM92/ref=la_B07211P1NS_1_9?s=books&ie=UTF8&qid=1499524891&sr=1-9&refinements=p_82%3AB07211P1NS

9) **Stocks, Mutual Funds:the Start Up Guide on Stock Investing** https://www.amazon.com/Stocks-Mutual-Funds-Start-Investing-

ebook/dp/B00WOGXCDU/ref=la_B07211P1NS_1_6?s=books&ie=UTF8&qid=149952
4891&sr=1-6&refinements=p_82%3AB07211P1NS

10) **Aerobics, running & jogging: 30 Minutes a Day Burn Fat Workout for Middle Aged Men"!: Two most powerful ways to burn fat quickly!**

https://www.amazon.com/Aerobics-running-jogging-Minutes-powerful-
ebook/dp/B00WA9ESG6/ref=la_B07211P1NS_1_7?s=books&ie=UTF8&qid=149952
4891&sr=1-7&refinements=p_82%3AB07211P1NS

11) **Diamond Cut Six Packs: How To Develop Fantastic Abs**

https://www.amazon.com/Diamond-Cut-Six-Packs-Fantastic-
ebook/dp/B01E2OELVS/ref=la_B07211P1NS_1_8?s=books&ie=UTF8&qid=1499524
891&sr=1-8&refinements=p_82%3AB07211P1NS

12) **15 MOST POWERFUL FEATURES OF PIVOT TABLES!: Save Your Time With MS Excel!**

https://www.amazon.com/MOST-POWERFUL-FEATURES-PIVOT-TABLES-
ebook/dp/B074THF418/ref=sr_1_3?ie=UTF8&qid=1504594835&sr=8-
3&keywords=besedin

13) **20 Most Powerful Excel Conditional Formatting Techniques!: Save Your Time With MS Excel**

https://www.amazon.com/Powerful-Excel-Conditional-Formatting-Techniques-
ebook/dp/B074H9W6XJ/ref=sr_1_4?ie=UTF8&qid=1504594835&sr=8-
4&keywords=besedin

14) **Secrets of MS Excel VBA/Macros for Beginners: Save Your Time With Visual Basic Macros!**

https://www.amazon.com/Secrets-Excel-VBA-Macros-Beginners-
ebook/dp/B075GYBLWT/ref=sr_1_7?ie=UTF8&qid=1506057725&sr=8-
7&keywords=besedin

15) **Secrets of Business Plan Writing: Business Plan Template and Financial Model Included!**

https://www.amazon.com/Secrets-Business-Plan-Writing-Financial-
ebook/dp/B076GJK8T1/ref=sr_1_9?ie=UTF8&qid=1509858352&sr=8-
9&keywords=besedin

16) **Top Numerical Methods With Matlab For Beginners!**
**https://www.amazon.com/Top-Numerical-Methods-Matlab-Beginners-
ebook/dp/B078HZV7VJ/ref=sr_1_4?ie=UTF8&qid=1516703667&sr
=8-4&keywords=besedin**

17) **Secrets of Access Database Development and Programming!**
**https://www.amazon.com/Secrets-Access-Database-Development-
Programming-
ebook/dp/B0776FZVG6/ref=sr_1_3?ie=UTF8&qid=1516703667&sr
=8-3&keywords=besedin**

18) **MS Excel Bible: Save Your Time With MS Excel!: 8 Quality Excel Books in 1 Package**

https://www.amazon.com/MS-Excel-Bible-Quality-Package-ebook/dp/B077WGQPBN/ref=sr_1_14?ie=UTF8&qid=1516703667&sr=8-14&keywords=besedin

19)   Why Your Body Water Balance Is a Key to Health and Great Shape?

https://www.amazon.com/Water-Balance-Health-Great-Shape-ebook/dp/B0787WCQ4V/ref=sr_1_16?ie=UTF8&qid=1516703667&sr=8-16&keywords=besedin

20)   Top 20 MS Excel VBA Simulations!: VBA to Model Risk, Investments, Growth, Gambling, and Monte Carlo Analysis

https://www.amazon.com/Top-Excel-VBA-Simulations-Investments-ebook/dp/B077P52LK7/ref=sr_1_17?ie=UTF8&qid=1516703944&sr=8-17&keywords=besedin

21) Secrets of Building Successful Business Plan for Farm and Rural Business!

https://www.amazon.com/Secrets-Building-Successful-Business-Rural-ebook/dp/B077BZJ3JF/ref=sr_1_20?ie=UTF8&qid=1516703944&sr=8-20&keywords=besedin

22)   Secrets of VBA for Modelers: Developing Decision Support Systems with Microsoft Office Excel

https://www.amazon.com/Secrets-VBA-Modelers-Developing-Microsoft-ebook/dp/B0797S7TLM/ref=sr_1_15?ie=UTF8&qid=1516968735&sr=8-15&keywords=besedin

Thank You but Can I Ask you for a Favor?

Let me say thank you for downloading and reading my book. Hope you enjoyed it but you need to keep on learning to be perfect! If you enjoyed this book, found it useful or otherwise then I'd really grateful it if you would post a short review on Amazon. I read all the reviews personally so I can get your feedback and make this book even better.

Thanks for your support!

Made in the USA
Columbia, SC
17 February 2018